بسم الله الرحمن الرحيم

In the name of Allāh,

Most Gracious, Most Merciful.

SPIRITUAL INSIGHTS

The Threaded Pearls & Other Bā-ʿAlawī Treatises

SPIRITUAL INSIGHTS

The Threaded Pearls & Other Bā-ʿAlawī Treatises

Translated by

Mostafa al-Badawi

Edited by

Dr. Muhammad Isa Waley

IHYA

PUBLISHING

Printed in the United States of America
First Printing, 2020

ISBN 978-1-939256-06-5 (Softcover)
Library of Congress Control Number

Published by
IHYA PUBLISHING
P.O. Box 426
Alburtis, PA-18011
U.S.A.
www.ihyapublishing.com
info@ihyapublishing.com

Translated by Mostafa al-Badawi
Edited by Muhammad Isa Waley
Book design & typography ARM (www.whitethreadpress.com)

Distributed by
MUSLIM PUBLISHERS GROUP
www.mpgbooks.com
info@mpgbooks.com
+1 (844) 674-2665

Ihya Publishing is a non-profit 501(c)(3) publishing house.

This publication was made possible through the generous support of the Sharieff Foundation.

Contents

TRANSLITERATION KEY

ء (أ إ) ’ (A slight catch in the breath. It is also used to indicate where the *hamza* has been dropped from the beginning of a word.)

ا a, ā

ب b

ت t

ث th (Should be pronounced as the *th* in *thin* or *thirst*.)

ج j

ح ḥ (Tensely breathed *h* sound.)

خ kh (Pronounced like the *ch* in Scottish *loch* with the mouth hollowed to produce a full sound.)

د d

ذ dh (Should be pronounced as the *th* in *this* or *that*.)

ر r

ز z

س s

ش sh

ص ṣ (A heavy *s* pronounced far back in the mouth with the mouth hollowed to produce a full sound.)

ض ḍ (A heavy *d/dh* pronounced far back in the mouth with the mouth hollowed to produce a full sound.)

ط ṭ (A heavy *t* pronounced far back in the mouth with the mouth hollowed to produce a full sound.)

ظ ẓ (A heavy *dh* pronounced far back in the mouth with the mouth hollowed to produce a full sound.)

ع ʿ, ʿa, ʿi, ʿu (Pronounced from the throat.)

غ gh (Pronounced like a throaty French *r* with the mouth hollowed to produce a full sound.)

ف f

ق q (A guttural *q* sound with the mouth hollowed to produce a full sound.)

ك k

ل l

م m

ن n

و w, ū, u.

ه h

ي y, ī, i

ﷺ *Ṣalla ’Llāhu ʿalayhi wa sallam*—used following the mention of the Messenger Muḥammad, translated as, “May Allāh bless him and give him peace.”

ʿAlayhi ’l-salām—used following the mention of a prophet or messenger of Allāh, translated as, “May the peace of Allāh be upon him.”

Raḍiya ’Llāhu ʿanhu—used following the mention of a Companion of the Messenger ﷺ, translated as, “May Allāh be pleased with him.”

Raḍiya ’Llāhu ʿanhā—used following the mention of a pious female Companion or other pious individual, translated as, “May Allāh be pleased with her.”

Raḥimahu ’Llāh—used following the mention of a scholar or pious individual, translated as, “May Allāh have mercy on him.”

Raḥimahumu ’Llāh—used following the mention of more than one scholar or pious individual, translated as, “May Allāh have mercy on them.”

Preface

The Bā-ʿAlawī tradition is founded on mastery of the religious sciences, meticulous practice of their content, and their constant dissemination among the people, which is the 'general summons' addressed to every Muslim without distinction. Their primary concern is to raise the religious awareness and performance of the entire population, so that those who are unaware of the basics of their religion come to learn and practice them. This is why in ʿAlawī gatherings one finds all kinds of people: students of the religious sciences, of course, but also manual workers, craftsmen, merchants, university professors, architects, physicians, and soldiers. Embedded within this framework of basic teaching and discipline we find a second level of summons, the call for those who have learnt the basics and show some eagerness to learn more and practice with vigor and sincerity. Fueled by a love for God and His Prophet that is constantly fanned by the teachers in the hearts of their listeners, sincerity inevitably opens these hearts to the lights of the higher worlds so that a thirst for spiritual openings appears that drives seekers to search for the path leading them to God. It is only at this point that Sufism proper intervenes, for then will the general summons imperceptibly change into a more serious kind of practice and the ʿAlawī teacher begins, very gently and very gradually, to take the seeker along the Sufi Path. At this stage it will be appropriate to discourse on the details of the method of travelling the Path as Imām al-Ḥaddād explains them in his works. Every now and then the teachers will make veiled allusions to the spiritual openings of the saints and the secrets that become unveiled to them, just enough to arouse yearning and determination in the students. They never discourse on these matters explicitly or for very long; what is more, they forbid their disciples to read the works of those authors who do. Their declared position is, '*Jāhid tushāhid*!' 'Strive and you shall see!' They believe that the inward knowledge of the saints is not to be discussed openly, for there is a very real danger of it being misunderstood and misquoted, and thus sending many of the unqualified majority astray. This is why in their vast corpus of religious books it is very rare to come across works that discuss such subjects, and even those ones do so with much reticence.

Stating the ʿAlawī position on such matters, Imām al-Ḥaddād has said, 'Whenever it is possible to combine conformity with the Sacred Law (*Sharīʿa*) with inward reality (*Ḥaqīqa*), that is what should be done; otherwise, the Sacred Law takes precedence in all circumstances.'

We have collected in this book five short Sufi works, which exhibit different levels of depth in treating their subject. The first is a description of the ʿAlawī method and so contains little by way of inward revelations. The second displays a branch of knowledge that is necessary not only for travelers on the path but for all serious Muslims to master: the science of priorities, which is closely related to the science of principles. Although often considered not to be spiritually relevant, it is in fact the very basis of spirituality. This appears very clearly in *The Four Circles* of Ḥabīb ʿAbd al-Raḥmān Balfaqīh.

The third, also by Ḥabīb ʿAbd al-Raḥmān Balfaqīh, is an example of how to base one's position *vis a vis* the ambiguous utterances and practices of certain Sufis firmly on the Sacred Law, but without denying whatever truth lies hidden in them. As the author makes clear, some of the practices he discusses are to be rejected outright, whilst others may be accepted subject to certain conditions.

The fourth treatise displays with the usual ʿAlawī concision the full depth of spiritual knowledge that comes from direct contemplation, between which and indirect rational knowledge, even when based on intelligent well-informed thinking, there is absolutely no common measure. Ḥabīb al-Ḥasan ibn Ṣāliḥ al-Baḥr's *Prayer of the Drawn-Near* is an example of knowledge entirely derived from spiritual states.

Finally, in *The Seven Stages* Ḥabīb Aḥmad ibn Zayn al-Ḥabashī demonstrates how familiar to the ʿAlawī scholars is the concept of the correspondence between the various dimensions of reality which permits phenomena of the physical level to serve as pointers to realities of a higher order, in accordance with the principle that in God's creation the visible corresponds with, and thus points to, the invisible.

The Threaded Pearls

AN EXPOSITION OF THE METHOD

OF THE ʿALAWĪ SAYYIDS

ḤABĪB MUḤAMMAD

IBN ḤUSAYN AL-ḤABASHĪ

Translator's Introduction

Al-'Uqūd al-lu'lu'iyya fī bayān ṭarīqat al-Sāda al-'Alawiyya (The Threaded Pearls: An Exposition of the Method of the 'Alawī Sayyids) is a treatise devoted to the merits and principles informing the 'Alawī Method (*al-Ṭarīqa al-'Alawiyya*). Written in the thirteenth century of the *Hijra*, it spelled out what for 'Alawīs ought in principle to have been too well known to need reiteration. However, it seems that a reminder had indeed become necessary, for the same century produced at least one other such treatise, 'The Banner of Light' (*al-'Alam al-Nibrās*) by Ḥabīb 'Abd Allāh ibn 'Alawī al-'Aṭṭās[01]. Both quote at length from two older tracts: one by Ḥabīb Aḥmad ibn Zayn al-Ḥabashī, written during the lifetime of his teacher, Imām 'Abd Allāh al-Ḥaddād, and recording his utterances on the subject; and the other by another student of Imām al-Ḥaddād, Ḥabīb 'Abd al-Raḥmān Balfaqīh, author of the second and third treatises in this collection.

Imām 'Abd Allāh al-Ḥaddād brought about a major shift in the 'Alawī method, rendering it much easier for subsequent generations to practice. Being the Renewer (*Mujaddid*)[02] of his age, he adapted the strict method

---

01 *Al-'Alam al-nibrās fī al-tanbīh 'alā manhaj al-Sāda al-akyās* (The Banner of Light: drawing attention to the method of the sagacious Sayyids), by Ḥabīb 'Abd Allāh ibn 'Alawī al-'Aṭṭās. The author, who died in Ḥurayḍa in 1334/1916, studied with such great Ḥabā'ib as Aḥmad ibn Ḥasan al-'Aṭṭās, Aḥmad ibn Muḥammad al-Miḥḍār, and 'Alī ibn Muḥammad al-Ḥabashī. An English translation was included in *A Blessed Valley: Wadi Hadramawt and the 'Alawi Tradition*, Vol. I (Birmingham, UK: Guidance Media, 2013), p. 174.

02 *Mujaddid* means renewer, rejuvenator. The term originates in the *ḥadīth* stating that 'God shall raise every century in this Community those who will renew its religion for it.'

of his ancestors to the times, abrogating many of its conditions in favor of a milder version which he called the 'Method of the Companions of the Right Hand' (*Ṭarīqat Ahl al-Yamīn*), as distinct from the 'Method of the Drawn-Near' (*Ṭarīqat al-Muqarrabīn*), as he called his ancestors' approach. This process evidently called for redefinitions and clarifications, the result of which were the works of Ḥabīb Aḥmad ibn Zayn al-Ḥabashī and Ḥabīb ʿAbd al-Raḥmān Balfaqīh.

Since their time, spiritual resolution has weakened further and, drawn by worldly concerns, people have drifted farther away from the path, so that reminders of the merits of the ʿAlawī method, such as this work, were called for. Nowadays they constitute essential information for anyone interested in serious orthodox Sufi methodology.

The author, Ḥabīb Muḥammad ibn Ḥusayn al-Ḥabashī al-ʿAlawī, was born in Say'ūn, now the largest town of the Ḥaḍramawt valley, in 1213/1799. His name al-Ḥabashī (the Abyssinian), comes from one of his ancestors, Abū Bakr, a descendant of al-Faqīh al-Muqaddam[01], who came to be so called for having spent twenty years in Ethiopia, calling the people to Islam and teaching religious sciences. All the illustrious masters of the house of al-Ḥabashī are so named after him, while his brother received the title al-Shāṭirī, the Divider, or the Splitter, for having split his wealth in two and given half to his brother.

Sayyid Muḥammad al-Ḥabashī studied under numerous ʿAlawī masters, among them Ḥabīb al-Ḥasan ibn Ṣāliḥ al-Baḥr, author of the treatise on the spiritual depths of the ritual prayer in this book. He also studied under numerous masters in Northern Yemen and the Ḥijāz.

He became an indefatigable traveller around Ḥaḍramawt, teaching, counselling, and setting a good example. In the process he visited Shibām and spoke to two eminent members of the Ibn Sumayṭ family, requesting them to find him a wife sufficiently knowledgeable to be able to assist him in teaching the women, thus complementing the work of *daʿwa*[02] that he was doing among the men. He was already married, but needed a wife quali-

---

01 Al-Faqīh al-Muqaddam, the Foremost Jurist, is the honorary title of Shaykh Muḥammad ibn ʿAlī Bā-ʿAlawī, the great scholar and Knower by God who is regarded as the master of the ʿAlawī *Ṭarīqa*. See *A Blessed Valley*, Vol. I, p. 54.

02 *Daʿwa* means to invite, summon, or call someone. In this context it means inviting the people to the Good pleasure of God, which means inviting non-Muslims to Islam and calling Muslims to a more serious and sincere practice of their religion.

fied to assist him in his work. The two sayyids lost no time in choosing a bride for him, and then immediately spoke to her father on his behalf and secured his agreement to give her to him in marriage the very same day, without dowry or preparation of any kind. The Sharīfa, whose name was ʿAlawiyya, very soon proved to be precisely what her husband had wished for. She went on to become a great saint in her own right and she bore him several sons, including the illustrious Imām ʿAlī ibn Muḥammad al-Ḥabashī, author of the famous *Mawlid* and a multitude of poems that are still the delight of Sufi gatherings to this day. His elder brother, Ḥabīb Ḥusayn ibn Muḥammad al-Ḥabashī, who like his father became Shāfiʿī *Muftī*[01] of Makka, died in 1330/1912 and was buried there, at the Maʿlā Cemetery. Ḥabīb Muḥammad was said by Ḥabīb Abū Bakr al-ʿAṭṭās, the Pole of his time, to have reached the 'tenth Station', which is the uppermost degree in sanctity and direct knowledge. In 1266/1850 he moved to Makka where four years later he was made *Muftī* of the Shāfiʿīs, retaining that office until his death in 1281/1863. He was buried at the Maʿlā Cemetery, in the *Ḥawṭa* or special enclosure of the ʿAlawīs.

As the translation proceeded we were forced to omit a few verses of poetry, mostly from the *Rashafāt* of Ḥabīb ʿAbd al-Raḥmān Balfaqīh, in cases where they were found too difficult to translate with sufficient accuracy and where they only served to confirm the preceding statements of the author, so that their omission detracted little from the meaning.

---

01 A *Muftī* is an expert in jurisprudence officially appointed to issue legal verdicts or *fatwā* and answer all questions pertaining to the Sacred Law.

AN EXPOSITION OF THE METHOD OF THE ʿALAWĪ SAYYIDS

In the Name of God, Most Merciful and Compassionate

All praise belongs to God, who has made the path of the ʿAlawī sayyids[01] one of the easiest paths leading to the manifest Opening, as well as the best and straightest of paths for both travelers and arrivers[02], based on the Book of God, the Sunna of His Messenger, and following the rightly-guided successors.

I testify that there is no god save God, Alone, having no associates, the Mighty, the Invincible; and I testify that our Master Muḥammad is His Servant and Messenger, the Leader of the First and the Last, who said, *Cling to my Sunna and that of the rightly-guided successors*[03] *after me*[1]. May God's blessings and peace be upon him and Companions who established

01 The ʿAlawīs were named after their ancestor ʿAlawī ibn ʿUbayd Allāh ibn al-Muhājir. They are also named Banī ʿAlawī, the Children of ʿAlawī, for the same reason. For Imām Aḥmad ibn ʿĪsā al-Muhājir, his son ʿUbayd Allāh, and grandson ʿAlawī, see *A Blessed Valley*, Vol. I, p. 46–50. The ʿAlawīs are also often called Bā-ʿAlawī according to the Ḥaḍramī local custom of changing Banī into Bā, and much less often changing the Bā into Abū or Abī ʿAlawī, all of which are used as equivalent in the present treatise.

02 A traveler is someone who is following the method of the Sufis and advancing along their path, while an arriver is a traveler who has reached the first degree of arrival to the Divine Presence, which is the state of extinction or *fanā'*.

03 The 'rightly-guided successors' or 'deputies' are the scholars who receive the knowledge of Revelation transmitted by the Prophet ﷺ, to the Companions, from them to the Followers, then to the Followers of the Followers, then to subsequent generations of upright scholarly men who continued to propagate this knowledge and set a good example to be emulated by the rest of the Community.

the foundations of religion, and upon their followers and those leaders of religion who follow them until the Last Day.

To proceed: The path of the truth is easy to follow for the God-fearing; for those who follow the guidance of the virtuous Predecessors, that which is remote becomes near[01]; and for those who avoid whatever may contradict it, namely the errors of *bidʿa* (innovation), its good is abundant.

It is as the Pole of Guidance, our master Ḥabīb ʿAbd Allāh al-Ḥaddād has said, 'Truth is too clear to require proof, and error is too manifest to be followed by those of the faithful who 'see by the Light of God', have realized the realities of certainty and excellence and are firmly grounded in knowledge, and for whom the unequivocal truth is unveiled by contemplation and direct vision. They are those who have purified their inward being of every vice and adorned it with every virtue, and purified their outward being by abstaining from all that is prohibited and performing all that is enjoined. This is the path which leads those who follow it to the locations of realization.' [End of quotation]

Know, O reader of these statements, that I have been asked about the method of the Banī ʿAlawī sayyids, the descendants of ʿUbayd Allāh son of Aḥmad ibn ʿĪsā al-Muhājir, so I assembled what I could find of their utterances on the subject and here present them to you, asking God that whoever reads them may benefit from them and that whoever reflects and ponders upon them may not diverge from them. I also ask God to grant me and them success. *Āmīn*!

Shaykh ʿAbd Allāh ibn Aḥmad Bā-Sawdān[02], in his commentary on the treatise by Ḥabīb Aḥmad ibn Zayn al-Ḥabashī, after mentioning what the Bā-ʿAlawīs have said in praise of Imām al-Ghazālī, says, 'Know that everything that the Bā-ʿAlawī sayyids have said in praise of that imām and his books applies to them equally well and to their books in which they follow his pattern, such as the books of our master the Pole, the Shaykh,

---

01 Direct knowledge of God and direct vision of the Light of the Prophet seem extremely remote goals to aim at for most people. Following in the footsteps of the virtuous Predecessors brings these goals nearer and turns them into realistic expectations.

02 Shaykh ʿAbd Allāh ibn Aḥmad Bā-Sawdān al-Kindī was a well-known scholar and Sufi whose spiritual master was Ḥabīb ʿUmar al-Bār Bā-ʿAlawī, Imām al-Ḥaddād's disciple. Shaykh ʿAbd Allāh lived and taught in the village of Khurayba in the Dawʿan Valley where he died and was buried in 1266/1850. Two of his works are mentioned in this treatise: *Fayḍ al-asrār* and his commentary on the *Rātib* of Imām al-Ḥaddād.

ʿAbd Allāh al-Ḥaddād ʿAlawī and others. They distinguished themselves from others and became famous for their *takhalluq* (taking on the qualities), *taʿalluq* (attachment) and *taḥaqquq* (realization) of the books of this imām, in *taḥallī* (adorning oneself), *takhallī* (divestment), *irshād* (guidance) and *daʿwa* (summoning to God), until their *ṭarīqa* (method) became one whose landmarks are clearer than most, capable of taking one to the Lord, the Master. Theirs is the most abundant share and greatest draught in following their ancestor—may God's blessings and peace be upon him.'

Our master, the very learned scholar and Knower[01], Ḥabīb Muḥammad ibn Zayn Sumayṭ ʿAlawī, in his book, *Ghāyat al-qaṣd wa al-murād fi manāqib al-Shaykh ʿAbd Allāh al-Ḥaddād*[02], writes on the authority of the venerable Sayyid, ʿAbd al-Raḥmān ibn ʿAlī[03], a descendant of Shaykh ʿAbd al-Raḥmān al-Saqqāf, that he heard Imām ʿAbd Allāh ibn ʿAlawī al-Ḥaddād one day speak in response to remarks made concerning the Path, its rules, and the innovations that had been introduced into it. Imām al-Ḥaddād spoke at length about the path of the Bā-ʿAlawīs, praised and lauded it in abundance, and then said, 'The Way of the Bā-ʿAlawīs is the most upright and moderate of ways and their behavior the best and most ideal, for they are on the exemplary path, the widest, best paved road, the clearest pattern, the safest, most beneficial and most upright of ways.' He also said, may God be pleased with him, 'It does not befit any member of the family of Abī-ʿAlawī to contradict the pattern of their ancestors, or to swerve from their path and manners, or to follow and hand over their fate to anyone who claims *taslīk* and *taḥkīm*[04], but whose behavior and method are unlike theirs.

---

01 An *ʿĀrif bi-Llāh* or Knower by God is a saint who has traveled along the Sufi path so far that he sees, hears, moves, and acts no longer by his own power but by God's. His human senses are greatly enhanced; he perceives by God's power, not his own, so that he can perceive much that others cannot and the subtle dimensions that they cannot penetrate. His heart is given an opening onto the higher worlds and more importantly, he is able to contemplate the Divine Names and Attributes by direct experience.

02 *The Ultimate Aim and Desire: The Merits of Shaykh ʿAbd Allāh al-Ḥaddād* is the biography of the Imām by his disciple Ḥabīb Muḥammad ibn Zayn ibn Sumayṭ.

03 Sayyid ʿAbd al-Raḥmān ibn ʿAlī ibn ʿUmar was Imām al-Ḥaddād's student and son-in-law. He died aged less than forty in the vicinity of Taʿiz in Northern Yemen in 1114 AH/1703 CE, while returning from *Ḥajj*.

04 *Taslīk* is for the spiritual master to take his disciple along stages of the Sufi path. *Taḥkīm* is for the master to accept the disciple's oath of allegiance to his particular

For their method is something the soundness of which is borne witness to by the august Book [of God], the noble *Sunna* [of the Prophet], and the well-pleasing pattern [of the Companions and Followers], as well as what is known of the ways of their noble ancestors. For they were transmitted this, each generation from the previous one, to father from grandfather, up to the Prophet ﷺ. In this they vary; some are superior to others, some more perfect than others.' He also said, may God spread his benefit, 'It is appropriate and incumbent upon all who belong to the family of Abī 'Alawī to call people and lead them to their Path. It is not appropriate for them to abandon their Way and incline towards another unless it be purely for *baraka*, and on condition that they do not weaken their hold on the example of their ancestors and their reliance on it. Anyone from the family of Abī 'Alawī who leaves the Path of his ancestors, may God be pleased with them, and dons the garb of others, loses all *baraka* in his endeavor.' He also said, may God be pleased with him, 'There is no method which was not altered by its people, and into which confusion was not introduced that contradicts the guidance of their ancestors, save that of the family of Abī 'Alawī.' He remarked, may God be pleased with him, that the venerable Sayyid Muḥammad ibn 'Alawī[01] reproached another sayyid for giving his allegiance to a man of *taslīk* who was not a 'Alawī. Also, when Shaykh Bā-Rakwa[02] came to Tarīm intending to administer the oath and the *dhikr* to the sayyids in the manner that he used to, he saw in a dream our master, al-Faqīh al-Muqaddam, saying to him, 'Get out of this town and do not tempt my children!' and he fled. He also said, may God be pleased with him: 'It is not inconceivable that the Shaykhs of the family of Abī 'Alawī

Order, which implies that the disciple is willing to be entirely obedient to the master, whether or not he understands the purpose and wisdom of all his instructions.

01 Sayyid Muḥammad ibn 'Alawī al-Saqqāf was one of Imām al-Ḥaddād's masters, although they never met physically. He died in Makka in 1071/1660 and was buried near the tomb of the Lady Khadīja.

02 Shaykh 'Umar ibn 'Īsā Bā-Rakwa al-Samarqandī was a disciple of the great Shaykh Abū Bakr ibn Sālim. Later on he became a spiritual master in his own right, attached to the Qādirī *Ṭarīqa.* His manner of acquiring disciples was to look at people and teach them the *dhikr* of *Lā ilāha illā Llāh*. If they were drawn to repeat after him, this was a sign that they were indeed spiritually connected to him, and so he instructed them formally and accepted them in his *Ṭarīqa*. If they did not repeat after him, he took this to mean that they were not meant to be his disciples. He died in the village of al-Ghurfa.

and the great men of God among them will have a rank and a privileged position in the Hereafter that will belong to no one else, a superiority over other Shaykhs, because they remained [in this world] in such obscurity, lackluster, humility, weakness, and lack of renown, publicity, or celebrity, despite their very high ranks and majestic states; in this pattern, they stand differently than others.'

In the book, *Tabṣirat al-Walī bi-Ṭarīq al-Sāda Banī ʿAlawī*, (Enlightening God's Friend Concerning the Path of the Banī ʿAlawī Sayyids) which was received by the noble Sayyid, the Knower and great Shaykh, Ḥabīb Aḥmad ibn Zayn al-Ḥabashī ʿAlawī from our master, the Imām, the Succour of People and Lands[01], ʿAbd Allāh ibn ʿAlawī al-Ḥaddād Bā-ʿAlawī, may God spread their benefits, he writes, 'I have heard him (i.e. Imām al-Ḥaddād) say, 'God ﷻ says, **And assuredly you guide to a straight path, the path of God, to Whom belongs what is in the heavens and what is in the earth. Verily to God do all things return.**[2] So he, God's blessings and peace be upon him, guides, by the light of God the Exalted, those of His servants whom He will, those predestined by God to receive His solicitude, to the straight path, the **path of God, to Whom belongs what is in the heavens and what is in the earth. Verily to God do all things return**. This path is here indicated by the expression used to denote the near, visible thing, in His ﷻ saying, **And this is My path, straight, so follow it and follow not [other] paths, lest they disperse you from His path**[3]. It is that which is explained in the **Book to which falsehood never comes from before or behind, a sending down from the Wise, the Praiseworthy,** [4] and is clarified in the words, deeds, and approvals[02] of the Messenger of God, God's blessings and peace be upon him, in all that was observed of his behavior and character, and followed by the greatest among the Companions and the members of his household, then the virtuous among the Followers and those who followed them with excellence. This was transmitted by Imāms Abū Ṭālib al-Makkī in his *Qūt*, by Abū al-Qāsim al-Qushayrī in his *Risāla*[03], and by those who followed in their footsteps. Then it was

01 The title of the Supreme Pole is *al-Ghawth*, which means the 'Succor'. This title refers to his hidden function as deputy of the Blessed Prophet in being a 'Mercy to the Worlds'.

02 This is the legal definition of the *Sunna*, for a *Sunna* can be what the Prophet said, did, or approved of the words and deeds of his Companions.

03 *Qūt al-qulūb fī muʿāmalat al-Maḥbūb wa waṣf ṭarīq al-murīd ilā maqām al-tawḥīd*

analyzed and detailed, refined, recorded, classified, explained and revised by the Imām, the Proof of Islam, al-Ghazālī. This is the path of the Banī ʿAlawī Ḥusaynī Ḥaḍramī sayyids. They received it generation from generation, son from father, and bequeathed it to one another, beginning from al-Ḥusayn to Zayn al-ʿĀbidīn, al-Bāqir, al-Ṣādiq, and then to other great ancestors down to this day. This shows that the path of the Banī ʿAlawī sayyids is nothing other than the Book and Sunna. They are of **different degrees with God, and God observes what they do.**[5] In this matter some are of medium rank, some are perfect, and some more perfect. They are on the wide, well-paved road which leads to God the Exalted. Those who travel this path are sure to arrive, but their traveling differs. Some travel in its middle, and these are very rare; some walk on one side, some travel on the edge, and others by attaching themselves to the travelers. The path of the family of Bā-ʿAlawī sayyids has thus been shown to be the straight path of God. They are those whom God has favored with obedience to Him and His Messenger, and being in the company of **the Prophets, the ☒*iddīqūn*, the martyrs, and the virtuous, and the best of companions are those. That is the favor from God, and God is sufficient as a Knower**[6].' A path that differs from that of the family of Bā-ʿAlawī to the extent of contradicting it is one of the dispersing paths that scatter away from the path of God ﷻ, for the pivot of their method is the creed of the virtuous Predecessors, working to perfect soundness in God-fearing, detachment from the world, maintaining humility, close attachment to worshipping activities, continuous *awrād*[01], feeling fear, the perfection of certitude, good character, good intentions, the purification of the heart and that which is inwardly hidden, and the avoidance of both visible and invisible defects. The reality of the superior man and of him who is even more so can only be known to God [not to created beings]. God's Reckoning is His knowledge of His creation, for

---

is a famous book by Abū Ṭālib al-Makkī (who died in Makka in 386/996) generally considered to be the predecessor of Ghazālī's *Iḥyāʾ ʿulūm al-Dīn*. *Al-Risāla al-Qushayriyya*, one of the earliest and most famous authoritative treatises on Sufism, was written by Abū al-Qāsim ʿAbd al-Karīm ibn Hawāzin al-Qushayrī of Nīshāpūr in Khurāsān (northeastern Iran), who died in 465/1073.

01 *Awrād* is the plural of *wird*, from the root *w r d*, which means to come to a well to draw water. The Sufis use it to designate their regular devotions, usually in the form of litanies and invocations, but also in that of supererogatory ritual prayers or recitations of the Qur'ān.

none can encompass any of His knowledge save what He will. His Pedestal encompasses the heavens and the earth, and preserving them tires Him not; and He is the High, the Immense[7]. Nearness to Him, Transcendent is He, depends on how strong faith, certitude, and excellence are, on the correct performance of obligatory acts of worship, abundance of supererogatory practices, emulating the virtues of the Prophet ﷺ, who himself emulated the attributes of God, such as mercy, clemency, sovereignty over things, transcending imperfect attributes and freedom from them, granting security, knowledge of the reality of things, loftiness of degree, and all other most beautiful attributes. This is the clear truth. To discourse on it is but to clarify the truth, God willing—and to speak of [God's favor in granting] it, for boasting is disclaimed in religion by being disavowed by the Legislator of Religion ﷺ. Therefore, if anyone's intention [in acting or speaking is to boast], he will have intended something that has already been disavowed, for he ﷺ has said, *I am the master of the Children of Adam, and that is no boast.*[8] He thus disavowed boasting, affirmed the truth, disclosed God's favor, and spoke of it.' This is what I heard from our master and Shaykh, the Imām, the Sayyid the Ḥabīb, ʿAbd Allāh ibn ʿAlawī al-Ḥaddād Bā-ʿAlawī, the Ḥusaynī, the Sunnī, in such or very similar terms, at the mosque of al-Awwābīn on the afternoon of Tuesday the thirteenth day of the sacred month of Dhū al-Qaʿda, of the year 1109 AH (23 May 1698 CE).' End of summarized quotation from *Tabṣirat al-Walī*.

This was confirmed by our master, the aforementioned Ḥabīb, when he wrote, 'All praise belongs to God alone. That which the superior, eminent, noble Sayyid, Aḥmad son of the noble Sayyid, Zayn al-ʿAbidīn al-Ḥabashī ʿAlawī has understood of our discourse, then explained and clarified, is as he has expounded and explained. He is worthy of this and well qualified. May God make him a shooting star in the sky of summoning unto Him and guiding to His path, a star that illuminates the road for travelers and guides the perplexed. May he continue to rise and increase until he reaches the ultimate aim, accompanied by the graciousness of God, His protection, and complete support and guidance. To God the Transcendent and Exalted is the return and the end. To Him belong all gratitude and all praise. He is the Sovereign in this world and the next. May His blessings and peace be upon our Master and Lord Muḥammad, by whom God guided us, by whose auspiciousness and *baraka* He favored us with that with which He has favored us. We hope for more of His favors through His favor, for all favor is His and in His hand, and He is the One of immense favor. This was dictated by the poor servant, ʿAbd Allāh ibn ʿAlawī al-Ḥaddād ʿAlawī on the afternoon of Thursday the twelfth of the aforementioned month and year.'

In his commentary on the *ʿAyniyya*[01] our master al-Ḥabīb Aḥmad ibn Zayn says when he comes to the following verses:

They firmly upheld the pattern of
the Messenger and His Companions
And those who followed them,
so inquire and follow.
Resolutely take the path to the highest station,
follow the footsteps in earnest fervor.

'This means that they upheld and practiced with rectitude the *Sunna* of the Messenger of God ﷺ, his exemplary way, the pattern of his Companions who followed and emulated him, may God be pleased with them, and of those who came after them and emulated him ﷺ, with excellence. These fine qualities are evident and well known in the Bā-ʿAlawī sayyids, the Ḥusaynīs, the Ḥaḍramīs, the Fāṭimīs, both those whom the poet mentions by name, those of their ancestors and descendants whom he does not, or the remainder of the Bā-ʿAlawī family. They all, may God be pleased with them, tread the direct, upright way in following the Sunna, and in this they follow one another. They practice the Prophetic method, the Muḥammadan Sunna, and the lofty Sufi pattern, with powerful determination, mighty resolve, and sincerity. May God grant us to adhere to their ways and may He not deprive us of their *baraka*, by the dignity of their Ancestor, Leader and Guide to the Straight Path, may the best of blessings and peace be upon him.' [End of quotation from Ḥabīb Aḥmad.]

Mawlāna al-Ḥabīb ʿAbd Allāh al-Ḥaddād, may God spread his benefit, also said, 'In these times there remains no better method than that of the family of Bā-ʿAlawī. The people of Yemen have conceded this to them, despite their own *bidʿa* [being Zaydī Shīʿa], and the people of the Two

---

01 The *ʿAyniyya* is a long poem of Imām al-Ḥaddād on which he granted Ḥabīb Aḥmad ibn Zayn al-Ḥabashī permission to write a commentary. Ḥabīb Aḥmad ibn Zayn authored a 388-page commentary, and as instructed he wrote full biographies of all the Sufi masters mentioned in the poem, and wrote equally amply concerning the self-discipline and stages of the Sufi path, but was very brief and circumspect when it came to the spiritual secrets of the Knowers.

Sanctuaries[01] despite their own highly honourable position. Therefore, comparison of merits can be made only among themselves. Theirs is a Prophetic method and they take their *madad*[02] only from one another. When they receive *madad* from others, it will still be through one of them.' Our master ʿAbd Allāh also said, 'Our master, al-Faqīh al-Muqaddam and Shaykh ʿAbd al-Qādir al-Jīlānī[03] are both great Imāms, comprehensive Poles, and Sunnī *sharīfs*. Each is a superior man, one of the Foremost and the Drawn-Near. We more manifestly and profoundly benefit from and depend on Shaykh al-Faqīh al-Muqaddam, for he is the father and the Shaykh around whom everything revolves in this region, both for us and others. They are equal in rank, but the influence of our master al-Faqīh al-Muqaddam is more manifest in the Intermediary World. Similarly, Shaykh Abū Madyan[04] is a great, comprehensive Imām, who was also made Pole, as Knower saints have stated. The function of Pole was thus transferred from Shaykh ʿAbd al-Qādir to Shaykh Abū Madyan, to Shaykh al-Faqīh al-Muqaddam, in this order, but not in immediate succession, since many Poles have intervened between them, for the time intervals were long. God knows best the reality of things. Our master, the Shaykh, the Imām, ʿAbd al-Raḥmān ibn Muḥammad al-Saqqāf[05], said, 'We concede precedence to none over al-Faqīh al-Muqaddam, after the Companions, unless specific textual evidence exists as to his superiority, such as for Uways al-Qaranī for instance."[06]

The renowned Shaykh, the great virtuous scholar and jurist, the martyr, Aḥmad, son of the Shaykh ʿAbd Allāh ibn ʿAbd al-Raḥmān Balḥāj

---

01 The Two Noble Sanctuaries are those of Makka and Madina.

02 *Madad* means reinforcement, so that for example when an army unit commander asks his superior for reinforcement and he sends him extra troops, these are called *madad*. This is material reinforcement. Spiritual reinforcement is inward spiritual help from masters to disciples to assist them along the path.

03 Shaykh ʿAbd al-Qādir al-Jīlānī is the most famous Sufi master ever. He lived in Baghdad and died in 561 AH/1166 CE. Branches of his Order exist in practically every Muslim community in the world.

04 Shaykh Abū Madyan Shuʿayb ibn al-Ḥasan al-Tilimsānī was a famous Sufi master, originally from Andalusia, lived in North Africa, and died and was buried at Tlemcen in Algeria in 594 AH/1198 CE.

05 See *A Blessed Valley*, Vol. I, p. 70.

06 This means that after the generation of the Companions of the Prophet and certain eminent Followers such as Uways al-Qaranī, in the eyes of the Bā-ʿAlawīs none is superior to al-Faqīh al-Muqaddam.

Bā-Faḍl[01], may God the Exalted have mercy on him, said, 'I have travelled many lands, such as Makka the Venerable, Madina the Honourable, the Yemen which comforts, and elsewhere. I have seen many pilgrims come to the Sacred House of God from the corners of this land and from other faraway places, and I have asked many trustworthy people, but never did they mention and never did I find among the *sharīfs* such a family as that of Abī 'Alawī, nor such a method as theirs, as concerns rectitude and following the Book and Sunna.'

Shaykh 'Abd al-Qādir ibn Shaykh al-'Aydarūs wrote in his book *al-Nūr al-sāfir*[02], 'For they are the best of God's servants and the dearest to Him. He adorned them with following the radiant Sunna, together with their authentic lineage extending to the Lady [Fāṭima] al-Zahrā', this combination being precious and rare, that of being both *sharīf* and Sunnī[03]. They were also graced with [abundant acts of] devotion, knowledge, humility and detachment, so that [even] the least, and the most neglectful, of them is a Sunnī *sharīf*[04]. May God be pleased with them and cause us to profit from them. *Āmīn*!'

Our master Ḥabīb Ṭāhir ibn Ḥusayn ibn Ṭāhir 'Alawī[05] says in one of

01 Shaykh 'Abd Allāh ibn 'Abd al-Raḥmān Bā-Faḍl was the foremost Shāfi'ī jurist of his time in Ḥaḍramawt. He died in 918/1512. I have found no biographical data for his son, Aḥmad.

02 *Al-Nūr al-sāfir 'an akhbār al-qarn al-'āshir* (The Light that Reveals the Events of the Tenth Century), is a book by Sayyid 'Abd al-Qādir ibn Shaykh al-'Aydarūs (d. 1038/1629) that chronicles the most important events of Northern Yemen in the tenth century AH, including much information about the scholars and saints of that time.

03 The notion was spread in the early days of Islam, after the age of the Rightly-Guided Caliphs, that most *sharīfs* would be Shī'a by virtue of their natural disposition and as an emotional reaction to the persistently virulent persecution they were subjected to. However, if one looks at the various families of *sharīfs* after the spread of Islam one finds that the great majority were Sunnīs. The example at hand in this book is that of the 'Alawīs of Ḥaḍramawt, but we should also remember the vast numbers of Idrīsis in Morocco, innumerable families of *sharīfs* in Egypt, the Mīrghanīs of Sudan, the Jīlānīs of Iraq, and so on.

04 Meaning that even the least in rank among them possess the morals of a *sharīf* and the beliefs of a Sunnī.

05 Ḥabīb Ṭāhir ibn Ḥusayn ibn Ṭāhir and his brother Ḥabīb 'Abd Allāh ibn Ḥusayn ibn Ṭāhir were both great scholars and saints. Ḥabīb Ṭāhir studied under Imām al-Ḥaddād's grandson Aḥmad ibn Ḥasan, his sons 'Umar and 'Alawī, and other

the counsels he wrote to another ʿAlawī sayyid: 'I enjoin upon you and upon myself, and would [only] be satisfied with, strongly adhering to God-fearing in secret and in public. In secret it is to purify one's mind of blameworthy attributes and embellish it with honorable qualities. Publicly it is to obey commands and avoid things prohibited, as they are recorded and explained in the books of the pure *Sharīʿa*. The way to do this and achieve what has to be achieved is to study the religious sciences with sincere resolve and good intention. He who seeks them in any other way will be turned back; his path will be obstructed. The seeker of knowledge will not achieve his aim, nor will he win a praiseworthy station, unless he examines the ways of the virtuous Predecessors as concerns knowledge, works, and what they acquired and what they left out, then follows in their footsteps, takes from their lights, strives to the utmost to emulate and follow them, and guards himself against abandoning himself to vain neglect.

'The method of our ʿAlawī sayyid ancestors is that which is well-pleasing, tolerant, straight, easy and pure. There is no swerving in it, nor deviation, nor is there harm in it to oneself or to others. It is explained in those books which describe their illustrious example and radiant life stories, such as *al-Mashraʿ al-rawī, al-ʿIqd al-Nabawī*[01], and other such works on the merits of the Banī ʿAlawī. I therefore enjoin myself and my brother to become acquainted with these works, master their content, adopt their path in earnest, and add ourselves to their number. This is equivalent to keeping their company in some ways, and to emulating them. 'They are the People[02] whose companion never suffers wretchedness', grievance, or abandonment.

scholars, and then took as his spiritual master Ḥabīb ʿUmar ibn Saqqāf al-Saqqāf. He also learned from the scholars of the Two Sanctuaries. He died in Rabīʿ al-Awwal 1241/1825.

01 *Al-Mashraʿ al-rawī fi manāqib al-Sāda al-kirām Āl Abī ʿAlawī* (The Quenching Source on the Merits of the Abū ʿAlawī Family), by Sayyid Muḥammad ibn Abū Bakr al-Shillī Bā-ʿAlawī, contains biographies of every ʿAlawī of importance from their very beginning until the time of the author, who died in Makka in 1093/1682 at the age of 63 lunar years. *Al-ʿIqd al-Nabawī wa al-Sirr al-Muṣṭafawī*, (The Prophetic Necklace and Secret of the Chosen One) was written by Ḥabīb Shaykh ibn ʿAbd Allāh al-ʿAydarūs, who died at Ahmedabad, Gujarat, in 990/1582 aged 71, having spent thirty-two years in India.)

02 The People, *al-Qawm*, is the name the Sufis gave themselves a thousand years ago, referring to the *Ḥadīth Qudsī* that describes people who gather to remember God and which ends with the words, 'They are the people thanks to whom those who sit

As for the deviant, he will join his kind, even if different in appearance. 'A man is with those he loves,' here and in the Hereafter. We ask God to realize in us the love of His virtuous servants, His successful party, for He is the One to grant success; He guides whomsoever He will to the straightest path. All praise belongs to God, Lord of the Worlds.

'This was dictated by the man in need of His Lord, Ṭāhir ibn Ḥusayn ibn Ṭāhir, may God pardon them all. *Āmīn*!' (End of quotation. May God make us benefit from the author.)

Ḥabīb 'Abd Allāh al-Ḥaddād, may God make us benefit from him, wrote to one of his followers: 'Pursue the sciences of Ghazālī and those that resemble them in the way of Sufism and Jurisprudence, which are the sciences of *Sharīʿa*, the explicit teachings of the Book and Sunna, for therein lie safety and bounty. Beware of all else, for it may confuse a man in his traveling.'

He also wrote, may God spread his benefit, to another of his followers: 'We enjoin upon you, may God bless you, to be careful with your obligatory devotions, to recite the Qur'ān in abundance and do the same with the remembrance of God, alone. Strive to study the beneficial sciences: Jurisprudence and others. Keep the company of only the best of people, people of knowledge and obedience, and avoid the company of the frivolous and the distracted. Have set *awrād* of *dhikr* and *duʿā'* with which you persevere after the ritual prayers and every morning and evening.'

The same disciple asked him if he might learn from other Shaykhs. He answered, may God spread his benefit, 'There is no harm, providing that their method does not contradict ours, which we took verbally and practically from those whose company we kept. For the paths to God are numerous. Some resemble each other and some do not, the differences being in the form, not in the reality. However, the traveler needs to behave according to the form until such time as he transcends it and reaches the realities, before which there are many things he will have to do and experience.'

Shaykh 'Abd Allāh Bā-Sawdān says in his commentary on the *Rātib*, 'To speak of the method of our masters, the family of Abū 'Alawī, requires lengthy elaboration. I have mentioned some of that in my commentary on the poem of my master, Ḥabīb 'Umar al-Bār, from the utterances of Shaykh

---

with them shall never suffer wretchedness' (or 'damnation': *Hum al-qawm lā yashqā bihim jalīsuhum*). [Bukhārī, *Ṣaḥīḥ*, 6408; Muslim, *Ṣaḥīḥ*, 2689]

ʿAbd Allāh al-Ḥaddād and others who have discoursed and commented on its loftiness, specificity, exemplarity, excellence, and superiority, and their jealous restraining of those who are affiliated to it but then wish to attach themselves to another path. It happened once that a certain Shaykh from Yemen wished to initiate the aforementioned Ḥabīb, our Shaykh ʿUmar al-Bār, may God spread his benefit, into a Naqshbandī *Ṭarīqa*. The Ḥabīb met a Bā-ʿAlawī *majdhūb*[01], Sayyid Sālim ibn Ḥasan ibn Shaykh ibn Ismāʿīl[02], who at once quoted to him this verse of Shaykh ʿUmar al-Miḥḍār[03], may God make us benefit from him:

He who comes to us, then leaves our land
afflictions abound in his town.

Meaning that he who chooses a path other than ours, having first belonged to us, shall suffer many calamities. The same Ḥabīb ʿUmar al-Bār when in Baṣra went to visit a certain Shaykh who, on their first meeting, perceiving in him the lights of sanctity and receptivity, decided to initiate him into his *Ṭarīqa*. On his second visit he said to him, 'Your Shaykh is al-Ḥaddād. They have praised you strongly.' May God grant that we benefit from them and from all His virtuous servants.'[04] [End of quotation]

Ḥabīb ʿAbd Allāh al-Ḥaddād, may God reward him with the best of rewards, said, 'How good is the state of him who concentrates on God and His obedience to such an extent that he becomes unaware of the states of the people of these times which contradict the rightly-guided pattern of the virtuous Predecessors and deviate from their praiseworthy conduct!'

Shaykh ʿAbd Allāh Bā-Sawdān states in his commentary on the poem of Ḥabīb ʿUmar al-Bār[05], 'As for their exemplary method, meaning that of the Bā-ʿAlawīs, mention will be made of what it was graced with by way of realities and merits over other methods when we come to the poet's statement, may God sanctify his spirit:

---

01 A *majdhūb* is an ecstatic whose ordinary consciousness has been overcome by the influx of lights from the higher worlds.

02 No biographical data are available concerning this sayyid.

03 See *A Blessed Valley,* Vol. I, p. 91.

04 What the Shaykh means is that he had seen Imām al-Ḥaddād, either in a dream-vision or in *ʿĀlam al-Mithāl*, and had been told by him that Ḥabīb ʿUmar al-Bār was already being taken care of by his ʿAlawī masters and needed no further assistance.

05 See p.29 footnote 04.

I took from great masters
and noble superior Knowers

We shall also mention the special character of their method, the purity of their 'drinking-place', the perfection of their following [the Prophet and their ancestors], the greatness of their character, the excellence of their conduct, and other attributes which are evidence of the truth of their being heirs to the Ancestor, the Chosen One ﷺ. People from East to West are agreed as to their superiority and merit over all other members of the House of Prophethood, both the descendants of al-Ḥusayn and others, in sum and in detail.'

Our master, the Imām, Ḥāmid son of Shaykh 'Umar Ḥāmid Bā-ʿAlawī[01], may God sanctify their secrets, wrote to someone who had requested to be given the ʿAlawī *Ṭarīqa*, 'They are descendants [of the Prophet], Sunnī Ḥusaynī *sharīfs*;

Meeting any one of them makes you say, 'I have met their master.'
They are as the stars which the night traveler follows.

Many among them reach the ultimate aim and achieve the status of *mujtahid*[02]. Many of their ancestors were said to have reached the degree of 'Supreme Veracity' (*al-Ṣiddīqiyya al-kubrā*)[03]. They are the ones who adhere to the Book and Sunna and hold on to them very powerfully.'

He also said, may God spread his benefit, 'The truth is that connection with the Prophet ﷺ, together with strong attachment to *Ahl al-Sunna wa al-Jamāʿa*, is a great blessing surpassed only by that of Islam itself.

01 Ḥāmid ibn 'Umar ibn Ḥāmid al-Munaffir was a leading scholar and Sufi master whose father and first teacher was one of the most eminent disciples of Imām al-Ḥaddād. Imām Ḥāmid also studied under his maternal uncle, Ḥabīb ʿAbd al-Raḥmān Balfaqīh, Ḥabīb Ḥasan son of Imām al-Ḥaddād, and other students of Imām al-Ḥaddād. In turn he taught most of the next generation of ʿAlawī scholars. He died in 1209/1795.

02 A *mujtahid* is an independent scholar, one who has reached such mastery of all the religious sciences that he no longer needs to follow the school of any particular imam, since he has become an imam in his own right. In practice, however, latecomers who reach this level of mastery still ostensibly adhere to one of the four known schools of jurisprudence and do not start yet another school, to avoid creating sedition.

03 *Al-Ṣiddīqiyya al-kubrā*, the Degree of Supreme Veracity, is the highest degree of sanctity and reaches to just beneath the degree of Prophecy.

Praise belongs to God in gratitude
for favors in quick succession
We praise Him silently and aloud
mornings and evenings.'

The author of *Fayḍ al-Asrār*[01] also reports the following: 'Our master the authoritative Imām, the Knower, Ḥabīb 'Abd al-Raḥmān ibn 'Abd Allāh Balfaqīh 'Alawī, was asked about the path of the sayyids, the family of Bā-'Alawī: what is it, how is it, is it enough to define it by saying that it is simply to follow the Book and Sunna? Are there differences among themselves or between them and other *ṭarīqas*? He replied, may God be pleased with him, 'Know that the path of the sayyids of the family of Bā-'Alawī is one of the Sufi paths based upon following the Book and Sunna. Its most important feature is sincere poverty and the acknowledgment of favor[02]. It is therefore to 'follow in a special way what the Book and Sunna say'[03] and to refine the bases so as to shorten the way to arrival. Thus it has an obvious usefulness and benefit that go beyond the common manner of following the Book and Sunna. This is because knowledge of the rules of the outward aspect of Islam is a basic matter, the content of which is general and concerns everyone. It includes all that is necessary to maintain order and restrain the base, as well as other common people. It is indisputable that people differ in their practice of religion according to the differences in their degrees. Therefore, there needs to be a knowledge confined to special people, which in this case is the special perspective of the élite concerning the reality of God-fearing and the realization of sincerity. It is a straight path, narrower than a hair and sharper than a sword, where the common teaching does not suffice, for there is a need for specific explanations and

---

01 *Fayḍ al-asrār bi-sharḥ Silsilat al-Ḥabīb 'Umar ibn 'Abd al-Raḥmān al-Bār* (The Effusion of Secrets, a Commentary on the 'Chain' of Ḥabīb 'Umar ibn 'Abd al-Raḥmān al-Bār. The *Silsila* or 'Chain' of Ḥabīb 'Umar al-Bār is a poem listing and describing all his spiritual masters. The commentary in four volumes by Shaykh 'Abd Allāh Bā-Sawdān is extant in manuscript form but has not been published.

02 This means attributing all power and ability to God, none to oneself, and acknowledging the innumerable Divine favors showered on each of God's creatures in general, and on oneself in particular, at each instant.

03 The special way in question being to choose from the range offered by the Qur'ān and *Sunna* the pattern of behavior that is hardest on the ego and then conform to it with utter sincerity and determination.

enquiry into every detail. This is the science of Sufism, and to use it to travel to God ﷻ, is the path of the Sufis. Its outward aspect is knowledge; its practice—its inward aspect—is sincere concentration on God the Exalted using what pleases Him in a manner that pleases Him. It comprehends every lofty character trait from the Sunna, and excludes every base trait. Its aim is nearness to God ﷻ, and the God-given Opening (*al-Fatḥ al-Ilāhī*). It is thus a path of qualities, works, and the realization of the secrets, stations and states that men receive from men[01], by realization, tasting, action and receptivity, each according to his opening and the bounties and gifts [of God]. As I said in verse in the *Rashafāt*[02]:

He who has acquired all the sciences
yet has tasted none is but distracted, asleep
Fear for him what you fear for the aimless
at the experience of death and terror.
One obtains it from the bestowal of gifts
the overflow of favor that follows effort,
Not from storytelling or books
nor from verbal discourse.
Blessed is he who is well prepared,
from servitude to others freed.
From the fountain of sagacity he draws his wisdom
experiencing its moisture in his mind.
The dew that falls from her sealed cup
on the garden of the heart with sciences
Preserves reason from illusion
and releases the mind from the knot in the bond.

'Now that you are aware of this, know that the Path of the sayyids of the Bā-ʿAlawī family was woven upon this loom. Its outward aspect is the sciences of religion and acts of worship, its inward aspect is to realize the stations and states, and its courtesy is jealously to preserve all secrets from profanation. Its outward is thus what Imām al-Ghazālī has expounded:

---

01 A 'man' (*rajul*) in Sufi parlance is an accomplished traveler and a complete saint—of either gender.

02 *Al-Rashafāt* (Sips), is a collection of Sufi poems composed by Ḥabīb ʿAbd al-Raḥmān Balfaqīh for a group of Makkan friends who had requested him to explain to them the main elements of the Sufi Path.

knowledge and action according to the upright manner; its inward is what the Shādhilīs have expounded, which is realizing exclusive concentration on *Tawḥīd*[01]. Their sciences are those of the 'People', their formalities are to erase all formality, and they strive to please God ﷻ, and draw nearer to Him by every kind of devotion. They approve of the *ʿahd* (oath of allegiance), *talqīn* (instruction in *dhikr*), *ilbās al-khirqa* (investiture with the patched robe), *khalwa* (retreat), *riyāḍa* (self-discipline), *mujāhada* (striving against the ego), and *ṣuḥba* (spiritual companionship). Most of their effort is in striving to purify the heart and preparing themselves by exposing themselves to the gifts of proximity on the path of wisdom and approaching God in every devotional manner, in the company of their guides. Besides sincere concentration for the sake of God, divine grace is necessary. Besides resolute striving and sincere effort, the opening from God is necessary. **Those who strive in Us We shall surely guide to Our paths; truly God is with those who act with excellence.**[9]

'The method of the sayyids of the family of Abū ʿAlawī is the Madyanī *Ṭarīqa*, the method of Shaykh Abū Madyan Shuʿayb, the North African[02]. Its Pole, the axis around which it revolves, is the *Fard*, the *Ghawth*, Shaykh al-Faqīh al-Muqaddam Muḥammad ibn ʿAlī Bā-ʿAlawī, the Ḥusaynī, the Ḥaḍramī. He received it from the men who had received it from those before them. It was bequeathed from great men of stations and states to great men. However, since it is a method of realization, tasting, and secrets, they preferred obscurity, anonymity, and exclusive instruction. Thus they refrained from writing or compiling, until the first generations went by, until the time of al-ʿAydarūs and his brother Shaykh ʿAlī[03], when the circle grew larger and so did the distances. The near and far became attached to them and this is when books became needed to provide explanations and definitions. There came forth, may God be praised, books which dilate the breast and delight the heart, such as *al-Kibrīt al-aḥmar*, *al-Juzʾ al-laṭīf*, *al-Maʿārij*, *al-Barqa*[04], and other works which soon became numerous and famous, well

---

01 *Tajrīd al-Tawḥīd* is to concentrate exclusively in *dhikr* on the formula of *Tawḥīd* and the Greatest Name, *Allāh*, and ascribe everything perceived in the universe to Divine Power alone. At a higher level it is to aim at the station of extinction in God or *fanāʾ*.

02 Shaykh Abū Madyan Shuʿayb.

03 See *A Blessed Valley*, Vol. I, p. 93, 94. p. 100–103.

04 *Al-Kibrīt al-aḥmar* ("The Red Sulphur"), *al-Juzʾ al-Laṭīf*, *al-Maʿārij*, *al-Barqa al-Mashīqa*.

known far and wide. This is why only the latecomers were prolific writers, and their works acquainted a vast audience with their way of travelling the Way, their experiences of stations and states following the exertion of effort and the influx of *wāridāt* and *jadhabāt*[01], their sciences of secrets and unveiling, in their behavior and utterances, ushering in the best of draughts[02] and the greatest of ranks. In this manner did their method become a well-defined independent method, its own light making it clearly visible, and in no need of being made known, since it had already become so to people of knowledge and had spread through their books and compilations. The virtuous ancestors had maintained their pattern, preferring to receive it by realization and works, which led to books on these sciences appearing only in the times of the followers of their followers, under the threat of losing what had been, in earlier days, so well known. This is the same pattern of the early Sufis who based their method on receiving it from each other, until *bidʿas* appeared and the threat of deliberate confusion, as al-Qushayrī indicates at the beginning of his Treatise. This is when the need arose for writing and the clarification of proofs. Shaykh Abū al-Ḥasan al-Shādhilī[03] was asked, 'Why do you not write about the Path?' He answered, 'My books are my followers.' It has been said that the Path of the Shādhilīs is contained in their litanies (*aḥzāb*), for they contain the realization of concentration exclusively on, and acquiring, the sciences of *Tawḥīd*, and sincerity in servitude [to God]. Among the Bā-ʿAlawī sayyids there are no differences in method; any apparent differences are due to differences in contemplation and unveiling. Some appear in Beauty, witnessing [divine] favor in its manifestations. They reveal their gifts, perceive doing this as permissible, and speak according to their expansive condition and spiritual

---

01 The literal meaning of *wārid*, plural *wāridāt*, from the root *w r d*, ('to arrive'), is one who approaches a well to draw water. The Sufis use the term to designate that which arrives from the higher worlds, whether it consists of inspirations, spiritual states, or other Divine gifts. *Jadhba* (plural *jadhabāt*), from the root *j dh b* (to pull), denotes the attractions of the higher worlds on the soul of the traveler; these can be of various strengths and last for any length of time: sometimes for seconds, sometimes for years.

02 'The best of draughts' is the descent of Divine lights into the cup that is the pure heart of the Knower by the grace of God.

03 Shaykh Abū al-Ḥasan al-Shādhilī was the founder of one of the most popular and widespread Sufi Orders, the Shādhilī Order. He died in the Eastern Desert of Egypt, while traveling for *Ḥajj*, in 656/1258.

state. The inward states of others appear outwardly as under the sway of Majesty. They request to be excused and relieved[01], and then persevere in following and remain in neediness and brokenness in all their acts and states. There is no difference between the two groups that needs to be emphasized, and no contradiction in reality.

'As for the Paths of sound, conforming Sufis other than the sayyids of the family of Abū ʿAlawī, they contradict them neither in their principles nor in the reality of travelling and arrival, the differences being only in formalities, organization, and 'drinking-places', all of which are due to their efforts in shortening the Path for the seeker. There is no divergence here more serious than the divergence in details between various schools of Jurisprudence. Since differences exist only in secondary things and fine ramifications, it is as if no differences existed in reality. Anyone who is impartial and enquires thoroughly will see that the truth is one, and will realize that there are no differences or contradictions between the people of Truth. Ramifications, even if numerous, all go back to the same root. God ﷻ says: **He has ordained for you as religion that which He enjoined upon Noah, that which We have revealed to you, and that which We enjoined upon Abraham, Moses and Jesus**[10]. **The Messenger believes in what has been sent down to him from his Lord, and so do the believers. They all believe in God, His Angels, His Books, and his Messengers. We make no distinction between any of His Messengers . . .** [11]. He ﷻ also says: **And when God made His pact with the Prophets: That I have given you Books and Wisdom; then there shall come to you a Messenger confirming what you possess, you shall believe in him and you shall help him. Do you agree?**[12] **We have revealed to you as We revealed to Noah, and the Prophets after him, and We revealed to Abraham, Ishmael, Isaac, Jacob, and the Tribes, Jesus and Job, Jonah and Aaron and Solomon, and We gave David Psalms.**[13]

'The reason they forbid a disciple, at the beginning of his path, to go from one *ṭarīqa* to another and from one Shaykh to another, is that this would be deleterious to him, since it would scatter his resolve and disperse his concentration. For his heart, at the beginning of his journey, is as if wounded, liable to be injured by changes and admixtures, until it recovers and heals at the hands of his physician, to whom he has become attached,

01 Excused from revealing their station and assuming the role of spiritual master, and relieved of the function of sitting with people to teach them.

who knows him, and who knows by experience the appropriate remedy for him.

'Perhaps God will grant me time enough to assemble the statements of our masters from the family of Abū-ʿAlawī on each of the subjects pertinent to the method, in such a manner as to please the people of direct knowledge. Success is through God. It is Him that we ask for help, in Him we trust, and on Him we depend.

'Dictated by the needy in God, ʿAbd al-Raḥmān ibn ʿAbd Allāh Balfaqīh Bā-ʿAlawī, may God Most High treat him with kindness.' This ends what we have copied verbatim concerning the realization of the secrets of what the ʿAlawī method contains by way of special attributes and merits." [End of quotation from *Fayḍ al-asrār*.]

Know that just as it is binding on the ʿAlawī sayyids to follow their exemplary method founded on the Book and radiant Sunna, so is it on all those who are attached to them and to whom they are attached, to adhere to it and never leave it for another. Shaykh ʿAbd Allāh Bā-Sawdān says near the end of *Fayḍ al-asrār*, 'When our master ʿUmar al-Bār says,

Hasten with resolve in the manner
of our ancestors, greatest of men.

'This verse specifies what is stated in general terms and in sum in the first verse. Here he asks His Lord, who never disappoints those who place their hopes in Him, to make him follow the most perfect of men ﷺ. But he lays down no conditions. He simply wishes to be granted to follow, no matter in which state, aspect, or path. Then he decides that it would be loftier and more profound to ask for the most perfect manner of doing so. For to elevate one's determination and concentrate one's intention on Him in whose Hand is the dominion of the heavens and earth, who possesses the keys to the Unseen, would be the mightiest and most exalted thing to do, since to elevate one's determination is an attribute of intelligent men of upright nature and sound make and character. This being so, our master the poet, may God sanctify his spirit, asks that his emulation of the Prophet ﷺ be of an especially perfect kind, difficult to attain save for those brilliant men to whom providential success is granted. This is to move with incessant resolve, driving oneself with various encouragements, according to the Book and Sunna, together with thorough emulation, while remaining wary of the threat of temptation. This is the path of his Knower ancestors, the striving leaders, descendants of ʿAlawī, son of ʿUbayd Allāh, son of Aḥmad the Emigrant to God (*al-Muhājir ilā Allāh*) son of ʿĪsā, who reside in Ḥaḍramawt and surrounding regions, and those who become attached to their path and enter their circle by becoming affiliated to them or they to them. They, may God spread their benefit, possess an exemplary method that comprehends all realization by following completely the Prophet ﷺ, and the perfect among his heirs such as the Rightly-Guided Caliphs, the greatest among the Companions and the Followers, such as [Imāms ʿAlī] Zayn al-ʿĀbidīn, [Muḥammad] al-Bāqir, [Jaʿfar] al-Ṣādiq, [Alī] al-ʿUrayḍī, and other members of the Pure House; and the likes of al-Ḥasan al-Baṣrī[01], al-Junayd ibn Muḥammad, the Master of the Faction[02], the Proof [of Islam] al-Ghazālī, the Imām of the [Shāfiʿī] school, Yaḥyā al-Nawawī[03], Abū Isḥāq al-Shīrāzī[04], and other such people. We have said a great deal about it, the advantages of entering the circle of its people, that which is special and exclusive to it in the way of measuring everything according to *Sharīʿa*, following to the full the Prophetic guidance, refraining from inventing anything that goes beyond that and arises from *istiḥsān*[05], and not adopting certain formalities that other Sufis have added. What we have quoted above from our masters Shaykh ʿAbd Allāh al-Ḥaddād, Shaykh ʿAbd al-Raḥmān Balfaqīh, may God spread their benefit, and other leaders

---

01 Al-Ḥasan ibn Abī al-Ḥasan al-Baṣrī was one of the most eminent Followers and a disciple of Imām ʿAlī ibn Abī Ṭālib. The great majority of Sufi Orders trace their attachment to Imām ʿAlī through him. He lived in Baṣra and died in 110/728.

02 Abū al-Qāsim al-Junayd ibn Muḥammad al-Baghdādī, also known as al-Qawārīrī, is one of the most important figures in the history of Sufism, for almost all Sufi Orders are descended from him. This is why he became known as *Sayyid al-Ṭāʾifa* (Master of the Faction). He was also a leading jurist, teaching according to the school of Imām Abū Thawr. He lived in Baghdad, where he died in 297/910.

03 Imām Yaḥyā ibn Sharaf al-Nawawī was a Syrian Traditionist and an outstanding jurist of the Shāfiʿī School. A prolific author, he lived in Damascus and died there, still in his forties, in 676/1277.

04 Abū Isḥāq Jamāl al-Dīn Ibrāhīm ibn ʿAlī al-Shīrāzī al-Fīrūzābādī was a major Shāfiʿī jurist and expert in the Principles of Jurisprudence. He died in 476/1083.

05 *Istiḥsān* means choosing the best option, and is used in the Principles of Jurisprudence to derive legal judgments, according to certain rules, in the absence of textual evidence from the Qurʾān, *ḥadīth*s, or utterances of the Companions. Here it seems that the author extends the meaning to include certain practices which have no basis in *Sharīʿa* and depend entirely on individual opinion.

in this field is sufficient and can be referred to.' [End of quotation from *Fayḍ al-asrār*.]

I have heard from a man attached to the ʿAlawīs that the teacher Shaykh Sālim ibn Sumayyir[01] said, 'Any of the ʿAlawī sayyids or other Ḥaḍramīs who takes a *Ṭarīqa* other than the Bā-ʿAlawīs' will either go mad or die'[02]. He then said that that a certain Ḥaḍramī man once took a non-ʿAlawī *Ṭarīqa* and went mad the same night. He also said that when another Ḥaḍramī took the Sanūsī *Ṭarīqa* he dreamed that it was Resurrection Day. He wanted to join the Sanūsī group but was prevented from doing so and was told, 'You are not one of us; you belong to the group of al-Faqīh al-Muqaddam.' The latter was then pointed out to him and he was told, 'That is his location.' He headed in that direction, found a vast crowd, and was able to join them. When he woke up he abandoned the Sanūsī Way and took that of the family of Bā-ʿAlawī. Such stories abound and are well known. We shall therefore leave it at that.

Our master Ḥabīb ʿAbd Allāh al-Ḥaddād says, may God be pleased with him and give us benefit through him: 'The method of the sayyids of the family of Abū ʿAlawī is to possess perfect beliefs, become attached to the Shaykh, receive the Shaykh's attention, and be refined by way of the inward. This is the method of the Predecessors such as al-Ḥasan al-Baṣrī and others.'

He also said, may God be pleased with him, 'We tread none other than the Greater Straight Path, which none can object to. It is the broad, well-paved way. God ﷻ says, *[Say. . .]* **This is my path, straight, so follow it and follow not [other] paths lest they disperse you from His Path.**[14] The paths meant here are the things that are obscure, so that those who follow them

---

01 Shaykh Sālim ibn Sumayyir was a follower and biographer of the great Ḥabīb al-Ḥasan ibn Ṣāliḥ al-Baḥr, author of the treatise entitled 'Prayer of the Drawn Near' in this book. Ibn Sumayyir was a scholar, a poet, and a judge. He died in Khalʿ Rāshid in 1262/1846.

02 This may be taken to mean that with such a well-established, demonstrably effective and superior tradition to adhere to, a man must either be mad or brewing up a madness to look elsewhere for his quest. However, even this should not be taken too literally since there are other *ṭarīqa*s in Ḥaḍramawt, as evidenced by the story of the Qādirī Shaykh Bā-Raqwa and how he was given permission to accept allegiance from the people of Tarīm but only for a limited period of time, and how a great Imām such as Ḥabīb ʿUmar ibn ʿAbd al-Raḥmān al-ʿAṭṭās accepted to take the *dhikr* from him.

are in danger of falling into *bidʿa*. Should one fall into *bidʿa* and be criticized, the critic cannot be blamed for it, unless he is moved by personal motives. He who objects to a virtuous man, making a legally sound objection that is mixed with personal motives, such as the wish to diminish and debase him in the eyes of others, will perish; but not if his objection is purely for *Sharīʿa's* sake and his outward behavior conforms with his inward feelings. Only in this manner will he be safe from the man he has objected to. It is said that Ibn al-Muqrī' was safe from Ibrāhīm al-Jabartī[01] only because he had no personal motives in his objection, it being purely for the sake of *Sharīʿa*.'

And he said, may God be pleased with him, 'He who comes through from the sayyids is pure gold, while he who comes through from the Bā-Faḍl is pure silver.'

And he said, may God be pleased with him and grant us to benefit from him, 'Anyone who reflects on the method of the family of Bā-ʿAlawī will know it is the middle moderate way, which cannot be objected to, whether as concerns their humility, detachment, poverty, anonymity, or their pure breasts. He who keeps the company of one of them must emulate him, even if partially and as circumstances of time and situation allow. Anyone who does not will separate from them for the wilderness, which means he will leave their path altogether, since he resembles them in nothing.'

He also said, may God be pleased with him and grant us to benefit from him, 'The spiritual station of our masters the Bā-ʿAlawīs is powerlessness, indigence and anonymity, in which things they differ from other saints. These attributes are an immense thing in drawing nearer to God ﷻ, and safety in religion.'

When a man came to Imām al-Ḥaddād asking to be given the Bā-ʿAlawī *Ṭarīqa* he answered him, 'Observe their actions, not their words; he who wants it should observe both their actions and their words'[02].

---

01 Ismāʿīl ibn Abū Bakr Ibn al-Muqrī' was a Yemeni scholar who lived in Zabīd. He became well known for his mastery of and writings on the sciences of Jurisprudence, Principles, History, and Arabic. He died in 837/1433. It is probably Shaykh Ismāʿīl ibn Ibrāhīm al-Jabartī who is meant here, since he was a Sufi Shaykh who also lived in Zabīd in the eighth century AH. He strongly promoted Ibn al-ʿArabī's teachings in the Yemen, thus attracting criticism from certain jurists.

02 The 'words' meant in the first instance are their claims that they are poor, ignorant, and neglectful, people of no consequence. To observe their acts is to see through this façade and see them for the scholarly saints that they are. The 'words' meant in

And he said, may God be pleased with him, 'The *madad* of the Bā-ʿAlawīs comes only from one among themselves. How many a well-known man lives by the *baraka* of one unknown! The sayyids used to live among the commoners, entering the markets and mixing with the people, passing totally unnoticed. When Shaykh ʿAbd Allāh al-ʿAydarūs became famous, he was blamed for it by the Bā-ʿAlawīs. The saint who lives as the commoners and mixes with them achieves mastery and increasing merit. God desired obscurity for them and they desired it for themselves, for what is taken away from this world is added to the next, and they were helped in this by destiny. They used to be called *al-riqqa*, which is the name of a tree that is swift to kill those who eat from it, the reason being that those who cheated or deprived them of something were soon afflicted.'

And he said, may God be pleased with him, 'The dealings of our masters, the family of Abū ʿAlawī, are based on the Sunna and on excellent customs; there is little good in those who neglect these.'

And he said, may God be pleased with him and grant us to benefit from him, to a certain Bā-ʿAlawī sayyid, 'The sayyids are pure, so do not soil yourself with sins; and they are hidden[01], their appearance being that of *Sharīʿa*, detachment, striving for God and concentration on Him[02]. Their house is inhabited, and that which is inhabited is not the same as that which is deserted. Al-Saqqāf[03] has said, "Our children are as those who dig in soft mud where water is near, whereas others are as those who dig at the foot of a mountain," or he may have said, "in barren, salty land".' And he said, may God be pleased with him, to a sayyid who was making an enquiry, 'The Bā-ʿAlawīs are only by their Shaykhs and their *awrād*. As for these [worldly] means, they are [confined to] to unavoidable necessities. He who abandons the way of his own people becomes like the crow who admired the way the grouse walked and wished to imitate it. When it was unable to, it reverted to its own walk but found it had forgotten it.

---

the second instance are their teachings on how to travel the path. These should be taken seriously by the seeker and acted upon without delay.

01 'Hidden' means in this context means that their inner attributes of sanctity and the spiritual gifts they receive from their Lord are hidden beneath an ordinary appearance.

02 This means that they appear to be somewhat upright and sincere common believers, their sanctity remaining hidden behind this façade.

03 For Shaykh ʿAbd al-Raḥmān ibn Muḥammad al-Saqqāf see *A Blessed Valley*, Vol. I, p. 70.

A crow wished to walk like the grouse,
having hopped along happily before that.
It fretted between this [walk] and that,
but could achieve neither this nor that.

A man is suited only to the Way of his people.' The sayyid he was speaking to said, 'I have grown distant from it.' He answered, 'You are still near to it, in fact you are following it; it is he who abandons it altogether who is outside it. **God changes not what is in a people until they change what is in themselves.**[15] A man has only to preserve his religion and his method. The method is nothing but recitation [of the Qur'an], *tasbīḥ*, and correctly performed ritual prayer. It is not that whenever he goes anywhere he should becomes distracted and forgetful, begin to talk nonsense and pray in an incorrect manner, or neglect his prayer altogether until its time runs out.'

And he said, may God be pleased with him, 'A venerable sayyid heard a *sharīf* say, "My father. . . and my ancestor. . ."'[01] So he told him, 'Be like your ancestor, or you will only be a tale and an image with nothing inside!"

Again, he said, may God be pleased with him and grant us to benefit from him, 'When a man praises and lauds himself by saying: 'We, I, my father was. . .' he diminishes in our esteem. We have neither respect for him nor trust in him, because Iblīs became hateful to God and was expelled from the Garden for a single utterance, his saying 'I am better than he[02].' This is not servitude but arrogance and haughtiness.' [End of quotation from *al-Fawā'id al-saniyya*.]

Ḥabīb ʿAlawī ibn Aḥmad ibn Ḥasan ibn al-Ḥabīb ʿAbd Allāh al-Ḥaddād[03] writes, in a tract on the pronunciation of the letter *Qāf*: "The Authoritative Imām, the Knower, the Traditionist (*muḥaddith*), Sayyid Muḥammad ibn ʿAlī Kharid Bā-ʿAlawī writes on the Bā-ʿAlawīs in his book, *Ghurar al-bahā' al-ḍawī*[04]: 'They are Ḥusaynī Sunnī *sharīfs*, of great worth among

---

01 The *sharīf* was boasting about the sanctity and good works of his father and other ancestors.

02 When Iblīs was commanded to prostrate himself before Adam he refused, objecting that he was better than him, being made of fire, subtle and shooting upwards, while Adam was made of clay, dense and thus subject to the downward pull of gravity.

03 Ḥabīb ʿAlawī ibn Aḥmad al-Ḥaddād, Imām al-Ḥaddād's great grandson, was a scholar and prolific writer. He died in Tarīm in 1232/1817.

04 Sayyid Muḥammad ibn ʿAlī ibn ʿAlawī Kharid, commonly pronounced Khirid, scholar and *ḥadīth* expert, author of *Ghurar al-bahā' al-ḍawī fī dhikr al-ʿulamā' min Banī Jadīd*

mankind on account of their rarity, according to the saying of Imām Sufyān al-Thawrī[01], may God have mercy on him, "Five things are rare. . .", one of [those things] being a Sunnī *sharīf*. The way of the above-mentioned people and of their descendants is Sunnī, and their character resembles that of the Prophet. Any impartial individual will recognize at once that they are true leaders, sayyids, *sharīfs*, because of the beauty of character and excellence of attributes that are theirs.'

'Then after enumerating a number of the merits of our masters the Bā-ʿAlawīs he says, may God have mercy on him, 'Be sure, may God have mercy on you—be certain in your heart and your purest conviction—that the Shaykhs I have mentioned in this book are all good examples and leaders. They are perfect and possessed of the mastery of the role of guidance and its lights, and the suns of the lights of *Ḥaqīqa* and its crowns. They have combined *Sharīʿa* and its different pathways with drinking from the purest beverages of *Ḥaqīqa*. They were given diverse sciences and inspirations such as were never arraigned for others. They were given the perfection of their Prophetic lineage and of their sublime inward knowledge and spiritual secrets, together with perfection of purity and freedom from any kind of innovations and egotistic motives. They were also given perfection in following the Book and Sunna and comprehension of the Aḥmadī heritage and Muḥammadan prescriptions. How many an ailing person has been cured by looking at them, how many a sterile person has become impregnated with their secret[02]! Those who are attached to and believe in them will find the horses of their spiritual power saddled, bridled and ready. On the other hand, ill-thinking, objection, and lack of courtesy towards them will be

---

wa Baṣrī wa ʿAlawī (The Blazes of Radiant Splendor, on the Learned among the Children of Jadīd, Baṣrī, and ʿAlawī). As its title indicates, the book is a compilation of biographies of the more important scholars among the descendants of the three sons of Imām ʿUbayd Allāh ibn Aḥmad al-Muhājir. Sayyid Muḥammad ibn ʿAlī died at Tarīm in 960/1663.

01 Imām Sufyān al-Thawrī, a Follower renowned for his erudition and piety, died in 161/778.

02 Spiritual impregnation comes about by the influence of the dominant, active spirit of the master on the passive spirit of the disciple. The result is the deposition of a germ of light in the latter's heart which, if nurtured with self-discipline and spiritual exercises, grows to full term and results in the birth of direct knowledge (*maʿrifa*) within that heart.

found to be flames that burn. For those who do not give them due respect and who object to them, they are lethal poison.'

'Shaykh ʿAbd al-Raḥmān, son of Shaykh ʿAlī ibn Abū Bakr ʿAlawī[01] told me, 'I heard my father ʿAlī say, 'I have seen the elders of the Bā-ʿAlawīs. Never did the moustache of one of them begin to appear without him already possessing [spiritual] unveiling."

'The authoritative imām, Muḥammad ibn ʿUmar Baḥraq[02], says that according to his Shaykh, the great scholar and Knower, Muḥammad ibn Aḥmad Bā-Jarfīl[03], the *Ahl al-Bayt* are the best of all people—and the Bā-ʿAlawīs are the best of *Ahl al-Bayt* for their following the Sunna and for that which has become so well-known about them and acknowledged by everyone concerning their knowledge, [pattern of] worship, good character, generosity and God-fearing.

'I once read in the *fatāwā*[04] of Imām Muḥammad ibn Abī Bakr al-Ashkhar[05], Ibn Ḥajar's disciple, that if someone wished to bequeath something to the noblest among the descendants of al-Ḥasan and al-Ḥusayn[06], one would have to take into consideration [apart from physical lineage] things of a non-physical order such as knowledge or *taqwā*. And God knows best.

'I also read a *fatwā* of Imām Ibn Ḥajar[07], may God have mercy on him, when he was asked, may God spread his benefit, 'Who is superior to the other, the *sharīf* or the scholar? Which of the two is more worthy of respect? If they meet in one place and something like coffee is offered to them, who should be served first? If someone wishes to kiss their hands,

---

01 Shaykh ʿAbd al-Raḥmān ibn ʿAlī ibn Abū Bakr al-Sakrān was a great scholar and saint who lived at Tarīm and died in 923/1517.

02 Muḥammad ibn ʿUmar Baḥraq was a well-known Ḥaḍramī scholar who died in 930/1524.

03 Shaykh Muḥammad ibn ʿAlī Bā-Jarfīl, a great scholar and Knower by God from the Dawʿān valley, was a contemporary of the great Shaykh Abū Bakr ibn ʿAbd Allāh al-ʿAydarūs of Aden.

04 Plural of *fatwā*: legal verdict.

05 Imām Muḥammad ibn Abī Bakr al-Ashkhar was the foremost scholar and jurist of his time in Zabīd. He died in 991/1583.

06 This is a matter of Jurisprudence. The heir must fit the condition stipulated in the will—that is, combine nobility of lineage with that of knowledge and piety—in order to receive his heritage.

07 Imām Aḥmad ibn Ḥajar al-Haytamī, a great Egyptian Shāfiʿī jurist, sometimes called al-Makkī because he died in Makka (in 974 /1566).

with whose should he start? We mean by *sharīf* a descendant of one of the two Ḥasans,[01] may God enoble their countenances!' He answered, may God have mercy on him and raise his degree, 'Both possess great merit: the *sharīf* for belonging to a noble lineage which nothing can equal and about which a certain imām once said, 'I recognize nothing as equaling descent from the Messenger of God ﷺ'; and the scholar for his benefit to the Muslims and guidance of those who are astray. Scholars are heirs to the Prophets; they inherit their knowledge and sciences. It is therefore incumbent upon anyone to whom success is providentially granted to give both *sharīf* and scholar due respect and reverence. However, when they are together, one should begin with the *sharīf*, because the Prophet ﷺ said, *Give precedence to Quraysh*[02] *and do not precede it*[03], in reverence for the noble lineage." [End of quotation from Ḥabīb ʿAlawī ibn Aḥmad.]

Shaykh ʿAbd Allāh Bā-Sawdān says in *Fayḍ al-asrār,* quoting an unnamed scholar: 'Imāms have differed as to which was better, the dignity of knowledge or the dignity of Prophetic lineage. Some said the second was superior because essential, not contingent. I have read that my master the Knower Sayyid, ʿAbd al-Raḥmān ibn Muṣṭafā al-ʿAydarūs Bā-ʿAlawī,[04] may God sanctify his spirit, quoted a debate that had taken place between the upholders of the two opinions. In the course of the debate the upholder of the opinion that lineage was superior asked his opponent, 'Should a *sharīf* lose his mind, would he still be called a *sharīf*?' He was answered, 'Yes, he would still be called a *sharīf*.' He said, 'But if a scholar loses his mind he is no longer called a scholar!' At this point the argument was won and the difference between the essential and the contingent clarified. However, that is based on the assumption that essential nobility is not contingent in any way. Yet everything is purely a favor of God ﷻ.' [End of quotation from *Fayḍ al-asrār*]

The author of *al-ʿIqd al-Nabawī* states that the Bā-ʿAlawīs were called after their ancestor, ʿAlawī, the first to be given that name.

Ḥabīb ʿAbd Allāh ibn Ḥusayn ibn Ṭāhir[05] says, 'Know, may God have

---

01 Al-Ḥasan and al-Ḥusayn, Ḥusayn being the diminutive form of Ḥasan.

02 Quraysh is the tribe of the Blessed Prophet.

03 Aḥmad, *Musnad, Faḍā'il al-Ṣaḥāba*, 1066; Bazzār, *Musnad,* 465; Ibn Abī ʿĀṣim, *al-Sunna*, 1519, 1620.

04 See *A Blessed Valley,* Vol. I, p. 109–112.

05 Ḥabīb ʿAbd Allāh ibn Ḥusayn ibn Ṭāhir was a great scholar and saint, among whose

mercy on you, that the most truthful speech is that of God the Exalted and the best of guidance is the guidance of Muḥammad, God's blessings and peace be upon him and his Family and Companions. God ﷻ says, **Say: If you love God, follow me and God will love you and forgive your sins;**[16] and, **My mercy embraces all things, and I shall prescribe it for those who are God-fearing and pay the Zakāt, and those who do believe in Our Signs, those who follow the Messenger, the unlettered Prophet.**[17] And [the Prophet ﷺ] said, *Cling to my Sunna and that of the wise, rightly-guided successors after me!*[18] His example, God's blessings and peace be upon him, in his acts of worship, ordinary activities, various situations, utterances, deeds, and character is well known, being neither obscure nor hidden. He has left us upon the wide, white road, the tolerant primordial pattern, the night of which is as clear as its day. Follow it and do not invent new things, for all good lies in following and all evil lies in innovation. God ﷻ says: **And that is my path, straight, so follow it and follow not [other] paths lest they disperse you from His Path'**[19]. **'Whatever the Messenger gives you, take; whatever he forbids you, refrain from'**[20]. **'Obey God and obey the Messenger'**[21].

'His Companions followed in his footsteps, adhered to his Sunna and walked his path. Such were our masters Abū Bakr, ʿUmar, ʿUthmān and ʿAlī, al-Ḥasan and al-Ḥusayn, Fāṭima al-Zahrā', his pure wives, and the rest of the Companions, may God be pleased with them all. They were all just, upright, wise, and good. To this did the Book of God the Exalted bear witness, praising and lauding them. The Messenger of God ﷺ, also testified to this, praised and lauded them, and warned against dispraising or finding fault with them. He strongly rebuked and threatened those who would do so. Most of the Followers followed the pattern of the Companions, as did those who followed the Followers with excellence, such as our Imām al-Shāfiʿī, may God be pleased with him, Aḥmad, Mālik, and Abū Ḥanīfa[01], then those who continued the same pattern, walked the same path, and adhered to their ways, such as our masters the Sufis, may God be pleased

teachers was his elder brother Ḥabīb Ṭāhir. He died in the village of al-Masīla in 1272/1856.

01 These are the founders of the four Sunnī schools of Jurisprudence, starting with Imām Abū Ḥanīfa, followed by Mālik, then al-Shāfiʿī, and finally Aḥmad ibn Ḥanbal. May Allah be pleased with them all.

with them all. These are the majority[01], the group that will be saved[02], for they are those who follow the example of the Messenger of God ﷺ, and of his Companions, may God be pleased with them, the pattern that joins correct creed to upright wise conduct, without vilification or criticism of any of our masters, the Companions, may God be pleased with them, and bearing in mind that from this majority came innumerable *Aqṭāb*, *Awliyā'*, *Abdāl and Awtād*. These are the people of God-fearing and rectitude, *Ahl al-Sunna wa al-Jamāʿa*, the people who combine knowledge and action with humility, serenity, and modesty. They are devoid of rashness and greed, full of circumspection, truthfulness and sincerity. How many an attribute of excellence do they possess, how many a quality of perfection! That which no eye has ever seen, no ear ever heard and no mind ever thought of. They are God's elect (*Awliyā' Allāh*) by the testimony of the Messenger of God ﷺ, who said, *Those who when they are seen, God is remembered.*[03] When they are mentioned, mercy descends. They are 'the People whose companion is never wretched'. In their words light is evident, for every utterance comes forth clothed in the attribute of the heart from which it came.

'Our conduct and that of our fathers, forefathers, and ʿAlawī ancestors never strayed from the upright pattern, the straight path, since it was received by Sayyidunā ʿAlī ibn Abī Ṭālib, Sayyidatunā Khadīja bint Khuwaylid, Sayyidatunā Fāṭima al-Zahrā' al-Batūl and her two sons, Sayyidunā al-Ḥasan and Sayyidunā al-Ḥusayn, from the Messenger of God, God's blessings and peace be upon him. Those, may God be pleased with them, learned from the Messenger of God ﷺ, and were followed in their conduct, path, method and pattern by Sayyidunā ʿAlī ibn al-Ḥusayn, known as Zayn al-ʿAbidīn, followed by his son Muḥammad al-Bāqir, the

---

01 The Prophet ﷺ, said that in this [Muslim] Community the truth will always be with the majority, the majority meant here being that of authoritative scholars.

02 *Al-Firqa al-nājiya* ('The Group that will Saved). This is an allusion to the *ḥadīth* stating that just as the Jews and Christians split into numerous sects, so shall the Muslims divide into seventy-two or seventy-three sects, all of them in error except one, those who followed correctly the pattern of the Blessed Prophet himself and his Companions. It was inevitable that every sect should claim to be the orthodox group, but the argument in favor of the majority, the *Ahl al-Sunna wa al-Jamāʿa'*, is overwhelming.

03 The Prophet ﷺ once asked his Companions, *Shall I tell you who are the best amongst you?* They answered, 'Indeed, O Messenger of God!' He said, *Those who when they are seen, God is remembered.* [Bukhārī, *al-Adab al-mufrad*, 323; Aḥmad, *Musnad*, 27599.]

latter's son Jaʿfar al-Ṣādiq, his son ʿAlī al-ʿUrayḍī, his son Muḥammad ibn ʿAlī, his son ʿĪsā ibn Muḥammad, his son Aḥmad ibn ʿĪsā, his son ʿAbd Allāh ibn Aḥmad, his son ʿAlawī ibn ʿUbayd Allāh, his son Muḥammad ibn ʿAlawī, his son ʿAlawī ibn Muḥammad, his son ʿAlī ibn ʿAlawī, his son Muḥammad ibn ʿAlī, his son ʿAlī and his generation, then our master Muḥammad ibn ʿAlī, known as al-Faqīh al-Muqaddam, and his generation, his son ʿAlawī and his generation, his son ʿAlī ibn ʿAlawī and his generation, his son Muḥammad ibn ʿAlī Mawlā al-Dawīla and his generation, his son ʿAbd al-Raḥmān al-Saqqāf and his generation, his son Abū Bakr al-Sakrān[01] and his generation, his son ʿAbd Allāh al-ʿAydarūs and his generation, his son Abū Bakr al-ʿAdanī, Sayyid ʿAbd al-Raḥmān ibn ʿAlī and their generation, Sayyid ʿUmar ibn Muḥammad Bā-Shaybān ʿAlawī and his generation, Sayyid Abū Bakr ibn Sālim ʿAlawī and his generation, his son al-Ḥusayn ibn Abū Bakr and his generation, Sayyid ʿUmar ibn ʿAbd al-Raḥmān al-ʿAṭṭās ʿAlawī and his generation, Sayyid ʿAbd Allāh ibn ʿAlawī al-Ḥaddād and his generation, his son al-Ḥasan ibn ʿAbd Allāh and his generation, Sayyid al-Ḥāmid ibn ʿUmar ʿAlawī and his generation, Sayyid ʿUmar ibn Saqqāf and his generation. Then it was transmitted to the ʿAlawī sayyids alive today. Neither change nor deviation ever affected their ways and beliefs. They remained on the pure white road, the powerful method, the even Path. This is why you can observe that those of them who perform their obligatory devotions, avoid all that is prohibited, then draw nearer to God with supererogatory devotions and the avoidance of all that is discouraged, suspect, forbidden or merely neutral, then adorn themselves with excellence of character and attributes and divest themselves of vile character and attributes, upon them appear dazzling *karāmāt*[02], knowledge of the Unseen, and supernatural events in quantities such as many volumes could not contain. Bearing in mind that the real *karāma* is rectitude, and that they desire nothing else and aim at nothing beyond it. However, these signs appear to them to confirm that they are the heirs of the Messenger of God, God's blessings and peace be upon him, that this heritage is perfect and covers all situations, and that they are the ones who truly emulate him in his behavior and speech. They are the treasuries of subtleties and secrets,

01 See *A Blessed Valley*, Vol. I, p. 89.

02 *Karāmāt* is the plural of *karāma*, the literal meaning of which is honor and the religious meaning of which is charisma or a supernatural or miraculous event or power.

the source of wisdom and lights, the lovers of God, those who know Him and are unrestrained in His remembrance. By God, only a believer loves them and only a hypocrite detests them.' [End of quotation from Ḥabīb ʿAbd Allāh ibn Ḥusayn ibn Ṭāhir ʿAlawī.]

This is what God has made easy for us to assemble and transmit of what has been said about the ʿAlawī method. It is sufficient for its followers and those who wish for safety. May God's blessings and peace be upon our master Muḥammad, his family and Companions. All praise belongs to God, Lord of the Worlds.

Now know, you who have read what we have just quoted and recorded about the ʿAlawī method, that I have read the following concerning the Shādhilī method, written in that manner by a venerable trustworthy leading scholar of the Shāfiʿī school, and I shall quote it word for word and letter for letter. He said, may God be pleased with him and grant us to benefit from him, *Āmīn*:

'In the Name of God, Most Merciful and Compassionate. Praise belongs to God, Lord of the Worlds. May His blessings and peace be upon our master Muḥammad, his Family and all his Companions.

'To proceed: [there are] some shaykhs who have assumed the function of guidance in these times make things easy for the common people and tell them: 'You should take the Path! All you have to do is attend the *dhikr* sessions, after which you will not be prevented from attending to your day to day affairs; you must be aware of God in every movement of yours, every standstill, and remain dissatisfied with yourself in all situations. It will then not matter whether you eat coarse or fine food, or wear coarse or fine clothes. You will not need to exert any effort in increasing your ritual prayers and fasts, for the obligatory and regular supererogatory ones will suffice you.'

'What they say is correct—but not for the common people, only for accomplished Knowers. As for those common people to whom this is said, they are ignorant of the rules of ritual purification, prayer, and other acts of worship. They know nothing of the correct creed of *Tawḥīd* by means of which their faith is made sound. How, then, can they reach the station of vigilance, which is the station of excellence (*iḥsān*)? How can they be dissatisfied with themselves at all times, when they are immersed in their pleasures and appetites, ignorant of the rulings of *Fiqh* and of correct beliefs?

'They also tell them that the sciences of grammar, conjugation, semantics and rhetoric are useless; adding, to be more convincing, that this is especially true if those who study them become self-satisfied; a true statement by which falsehood is intended[01]. Their aim is to make these sciences repugnant to the people, lest by pursuing them they be prevented from joining them. Their saying that they are useless is a lie, a calumny and a falsehood. They make the common people believe that those who study these sciences are self-satisfied and therefore contemptible, which leads to their despising knowledge and scholars. How [dare they do this] when studying these sciences is a *kifāya* or collective obligation by consensus of all the leading scholars? For by them *Sharīʿa* is safeguarded, since it is in Arabic that it was revealed, and *Sharīʿa* is the [protective] wall surrounding *Ḥaqīqa*. Had the scholars not taken great pains with these sciences, they would have been unable to understand the subtleties of the Book and Sunna, so as to extract fine rulings from them, and the people of *bidʿa* and error would have manipulated these and destroyed *Sharīʿa*. How dare they frighten people away from these sciences, when they are the foundations of both *Sharīʿa* and *Ḥaqīqa*? It is said that when Imām Abū Isḥāq al-Shīrāzī[02] had had his fill of sciences, he wanted to devote himself to worship and to forsake human society. He heard a voice saying, 'Now that you have become God's Proof on His earth, do you desire to seclude yourself?' In his days heresies had become rife and heretics were sapping the very foundations of *Ahl al-Sunna* and disputing with them. He once climbed the mountain of Lebanon, where Sufis used to go to worship in Syria, and found many scholars in retreat there with the Sufis. He said to them, 'You grass-eaters, would Muḥammad, God's blessings and peace be upon him, be pleased to see you like this when heretics are snatching away his people and destroying his *Sharīʿa*?' He then ordered them to come down and resume their scholarly functions. A similar story is told of Imām al-Isfarāʾīnī[03].

'As for self-satisfaction, it is bad whether in a scholarly or an ignorant

---

01 This remark was originally made by Imām ʿAlī ibn Abī Ṭālib upon learning that his enemies (the Khawārij) were proclaiming that they accepted no authority and no judgement save that of 'God and His Book,' which in effect meant that they believed themselves to be more knowledgeable than Imām ʿAlī and the other Companions in understanding the Book of God and Sunna of His Prophet ﷺ.

02 See p. 37 footnote 04.

03 Imām Ṭāhir ibn Muḥammad al-Isfarāʾīnī was a leading theologian who also wrote on the differences between the various sects that appeared within the Muslim Community up until his time. He died in 471/1078.

man, but clearly worse in a scholar. However, where is it to be found that all those who study such sciences are self-satisfied? Many people can study them with sound intentions, especially if their aim is to use them to attain to the mastery of the knowledge of the Book, Sunna, and *Fiqh* for the purpose of shouldering the burden of *Sharīʿa* and defending it. They do this while maintaining their performance of obligations, avoidance of prohibitions, and dissatisfaction with themselves. How can the ignorant common man ever reach such a station? However, the aim of the shaykhs in question is to frighten people away from seeking knowledge and keeping the company of scholars, so that they may remain free to join them. They make things so easy for them that devils juggle with them and send them plummeting into the abysses of error, committing all sorts of debauchery and corruption while considering it sufficient to say, 'We are the people of the inward, those are the people of the outward. We are the people of *Ṭarīqa*, *Ḥaqīqa*, *murāqaba*, and presence with God ﷻ.' How could they be, when their earnings are *ḥarām* and they commit major sins, when their tongues are busy backbiting and slandering and their souls filled with blameworthy attributes, when they know nothing about disciplining one's character? On the contrary, they are by nature seditious and hypocrites. Arouse the anger of one of them for any trivial reason, and you will see incredible signs of his bad character and obscenity! That is not how the Companions were, or the virtuous Predecessors. These are but confusing tricks invented by heretics.

'One should mention that these shaykhs base their method of making things easy on the utterances of certain great Knowers who when they spoke were addressing people close to the station of direct knowledge, not ignorant transgressors. But these shaykhs take such statements and address them to the ignorant. They do not know that to each station its language and to each field its men. The Legislator has enjoined us to speak to each according to their understanding. He favored the great among his Companions, God's blessings and peace be upon him, with [spiritual] secrets, while addressing the rest of the Community with the outward aspect of *Sharīʿa*. The Predecessors, when they wished to discourse on *Ḥaqīqa*, shut the doors and pushed out anyone who had no aptitude for it. Among the things that those [false] shaykhs quote is the saying of Shaykh Abū al-Ḥasan al-Shādhilī, may God be pleased with him, 'He who leads you to works will have tired you out, but he who leads you to God will have been a good counselor to you.' These shaykhs deceive the common people into believing that the works and efforts expounded by Imām al-Ghazālī, may God be pleased with him, and others are useless and tiresome. They have not understood what the Shaykh meant, may God be pleased with him. What he intended by that statement is that he who leads you to works that are not coupled with treating the heart by removing blameworthy and acquiring praiseworthy attributes will have tired you out, but he who leads you to God, by knowledge and deeds, observing the defects of the soul, striving to remove blameworthy and acquire praiseworthy attributes, will have been of good counsel to you. That is what he meant, and this is confirmed by many Shādhilīs in their writings. He spoke succinctly, because he was addressing those whose understanding was complete and whose station was approaching that of direct spiritual knowledge. He did not address such words to ignorant reckless people. Other statements they cling to are the saying of al-Shādhilī, may God be pleased with him, 'All you have to do is obey orders, observe prohibitions, witness that all [thanks for] favors and all gratitude belong to God ﷻ; and be dissatisfied with yourself. It will not harm you then if your works be few!' and his saying, may God be pleased with him, 'A few works accompanied by witnessing the favor of God ﷻ are better than numerous works accompanied by witnessing one's shortcomings.' Such statements and other similar ones, uttered by him and many other Knowers, are true and undoubtedly so; but they are addressed to those who are approaching the station of direct spiritual knowledge, whose souls are neither immersed in pleasures nor occupied with contraventions. Such people would have spent their lives in acts of obedience, acquiring knowledge, and avoiding contraventions. Should they need help to reach God ﷻ, such statements will make things easier for them. As for those who are immersed in their appetites, as most people are, they should only be encouraged to exert serious effort, increase their acts of worship and take the hard path, until their souls become disciplined and docile. Imām al-Shādhilī himself, may God be pleased with him, stated as much on many occasions, as you will see. There is not much difference between his method and that of the Predecessors expounded by Imām al-Ghazālī, may God be pleased with him, in the *Iḥyā'* and other works. The pattern of the Predecessors is that which is suitable for both the common and the elect. He states on many occasions in the *Iḥyā'* that when the servant [of God] expels from his heart all that is not God ﷻ, and reaches the station of vigilance (*murāqaba*) and witnessing (*shuhūd*), and he witnesses the favors of God and renders thanks for them, while obeying orders and observing prohibitions, he may reach God ﷻ, in a flash. However, for most people this happens only after much effort, and its is very rare without it. Imām al-Shādhilī, may God be pleased with him, looked at times at those rare individuals and addressed them with these words. This does not mean that he disagrees with Imām al-Ghazālī in his exposition, since this is what is beneficial to the majority of people. He made clear statements to this effect, as you will see. A great Shādhilī Shaykh was asked, 'Is the method expounded by Imām al-Ghazālī better, or that which is well-known to be associated with Imām al-Shādhilī, which is expelling all that is not God from the heart, witnessing the favor of God, being thankful, obeying orders and avoiding prohibitions, without need for much works and effort?' He replied: 'We cannot say that one is unconditionally better than the other. We should say that what Imām al-Ghazālī has expounded is that which is beneficial to the majority of people, because of their immersion in appetites, while what Imām al-Shādhilī has said is beneficial to those who have spent their lifetimes in obedience, observing prohibitions, and only have a foot or two [more] to go to arrive. The former is more suited to some people, the latter to others. Both al-Ghazālī and al-Shādhilī agree on this. One can say that all the people of the Path agree on this and there is not one dissenter.'

'The proof for this is this saying of al-Shādhilī, may God be pleased with him, as recorded by al-Shaʿrānī in his *Ṭabaqāt*[01]: 'Any knowledge which when you study you find your own thoughts taking precedence over it, your ego attracted to it, and your nature finds it pleasurable, throw it away even if be true! Take the knowledge of God which He revealed to His Messenger ﷺ, follow him and the Caliphs, Companions, Followers, and the imāms who are free from being led by passions. In this manner you will be safe from the doubts, conjectures and false illusions that may lead you away from right guidance and its realities.' Reflect on this statement and you will find that it corresponds exactly to what Ghazālī has written.

'Al-Shādhilī, may God be pleased with him, also said, 'You will never catch as much as a whiff of the Path as long as you are not detached from

---

01 'Abd al-Wahhāb al-Shaʿrānī, a great Azharī scholar and Sufi saint, a prolific and influential writer, lived in Cairo, where he died in 973/1565. The book in question, *al-Ṭabaqāt al-Kubrā* (The Great Strata), is a compilation of biographies of Muslim saints from the first generation of the Companions of the Prophet ﷺ down to that of the author's contemporaries.

this world and its people.' He also said, may God be pleased with him, 'He who summons [people] to God in a manner other than that of the Messenger of God, may blessings and peace be upon him, is a heretic.' And he said, may God be pleased with him, 'Should a *faqīr* ever defend himself and answer back[01], he and dust become equal.'

'And he said, may God be pleased with him, 'He who desires dignity in this world and the Next, let him enter our school for a day or two.' He was asked, 'How can I do this?' He answered, 'Disperse the idols in your heart, give rest to your body from this world, then be as you please; for God will not chastise the servant for spreading his legs to rest while remaining humble, but He will chastise him for effort accompanied by arrogance.'

'And he said, may God be pleased with him, 'Nothing is more sinful according to us than these two things: to love this world and prefer oneself to others, and to remain satisfied with ignorance; for the love of this world is the precursor of every sin and remaining in ignorance the origin of every transgression.'

'And he said, may God be pleased with him, 'One cannot say that a servant has forsaken sins until they do not even cross his mind, for the reality of forsaking is to forget the thing forsaken. This applies to the perfect among men. As for those whose state is not thus, let them strive and exert serious effort.'

'Consider these words and you will find they conform exactly to what was expounded by Ghazālī; to each state its men.

'Shaykh Abū al-ʿAbbās al-Mursī[02], may God be pleased with him, said, 'Those among this group who perish outnumber those whom it saves. This is because they are excessively neglectful and leave its conditions unfulfilled.'

'And al-Shādhilī said, may God be pleased with him, 'If you wish to combat your ego (*jihād al-nafs*), impose upon it never to move save in accordance with religious knowledge. Lash it with fear before every step; imprison it in the fist of God ﷻ. Wherever you may be, complain to God

01 When the *faqīr* feels he has to stand up and defend himself against his critics or adversaries, this means that his ego is still very much alive and he is thus of no worth on the Path.

02 Shaykh Abū al-ʿAbbās al-Mursī was the foremost disciple and successor of Shaykh Abū al-Ḥasan al-Shādhilī. He hailed from Murcia in Spain, whence his name al-Mursī, but lived most of his life in Alexandria, Egypt, where he died and was buried in 686/1287.

about your powerlessness when you are distracted, for this ego that you cannot control is surrounded by God. Whenever it is made subservient to you in any matter, you should remember the favor of your Lord and say, **Transcendent is He who has subjected this to us, for we ourselves could never have subdued it.**'[22] And he said, may God be pleased with him, 'There are two all-comprehending, all-embracing *karāmāt*: the *karāma* of faith with great certitude and witnessing, and that of working in conformity and emulation, while avoiding boastfulness and deceit. He who is given these two and yet yearns for others is but a lying, false servant. He is like someone who is honored with seeing the king and serving under his contented gaze, yet yearns to look after animals.'

'And he said, may God be pleased with him, 'The high-ranking saint drives some people by knowledge, others by realities, and others by secrets. These [great men] are the deputies of the Prophets and the substitutes of the Messenger; they are the *Ṣiddīqūn*.'

'Consider how he differentiated between various means for guiding various people and did not impose the same pattern on all.

'A certain Shādhilī stated that if the novice is able to study the religious sciences and their tools then the Shaykh will allow him to do so and counsel him to make his intention sound and sincere, for he will then be preserving *Sharīʿa* and fulfilling a *kifāya* [collective] obligation. If his aptitude does not allow delving into such sciences, the Shaykh will counsel him to learn the necessary beliefs and rules, then keep to remembrance, reflection, and striving. He will not treat all disciples in the same manner, nor gather the ignorant and address them as he addresses Knowers, for this is a serious error that would lead to their despising both knowledge and the learned as well as acts of worship and worshipers.

'Says Ibn ʿAṭā' Allāh in *Laṭā'if al-Minan*[01], 'The Shaykh's method is built on union with God[02], avoiding separation, remembrance, reflection, and

01 Shaykh Aḥmad Ibn ʿAṭā' Allāh al-Iskandarī, successor of Shaykh Abū al-ʿAbbās al-Mursī at the head of the Shādhilī Order. He was an eminent Azharī teacher with numerous well-known works on Sufism, many of which are still widely read and taught today. *Laṭā'if al-minan* (Subtle Gift) is a book on the merits and teachings of his master, Shaykh Abū al-ʿAbbās al-Mursī, and the latter's master, Shaykh Abū al-Ḥasan al-Shādhilī. He died in Cairo in 709/1310.

02 'Union with God' in Sufi parlance means to remain permanently in the Divine Presence.

remaining in retreat. For each disciple he has a way, taking each by the route most suited to him.'

Consider this statement and you will find it conforms with what was said before.

Shaykh 'Abd al-Wāḥid al-Maghribī al-Shādhilī[01] authored a treatise on the Shādhilī Path and discoursed on it at length. He said that the path has three divisions and people are also divided into three according to their differences and variety of states, so that each has a path of his own.

'The first group comprises those whose constitution is dense and their understanding weak, and who find difficulty in learning and in comprehending subtle expressions. Their Path consists in worship and devotion, abundant fasts, prayers, recitations of the Qur'ān, *Ḥajj*, *Jihād*, and other outward works. This group can bear the burden of acts of worship and does not find them tedious; on the contrary, they easily make them a habit, just like ordinary activities. They will continue to ascend until they approach the location where inward knowledge alights, the glory of the Beloved is unveiled before them, and they witness the wonders of the Unseen.

'The second group possesses agile understanding, predatory character, fiery forms, and proud souls. Such are people in high position and rank, who pursue secondary causes and cannot control themselves when angry. Their Path is striving and self-discipline, changing their character, purifying their souls, and pursuing that which will reform their inward. They keep striving to erase whatever blameworthy attributes are imprinted on their souls until these disappear and the souls revert to their sound original nature. The most important thing here is to contradict the ego in its wishes and refuse it what it desires until it comes to find contentment no different from anger, rest from toil, position of power from the lowliest of ranks, or earning from not earning by abandoning all crafts and means. Then they will rejoin the group of the people of solicitude and election. This method is less dread-inspiring than the previous one, and those who arrive through it are the great men.

'The third group consists of those whose souls are contented, their minds pure and their nature essentially veracious. Their Way is that of those who travel to God, Exalted is He, by flying to Him. It is the Path of the Lovers.

---

01 Shaykh 'Abd al-Wāḥid al-Maghribī, a Mālikī scholar and physician of Damascus, died in 944/1537.

The most important thing to travel this path is purity of heart, sincerity in love, and outward and inward confirmation of love by every means. They renounce their ability, strength, intelligence and sagacity. Were they to be asked to give up their lives they would not find it difficult. It is then that the spirit of the nearness of contemplation is insufflated into them and they realize His saying, '**All that dwells upon the Earth is perishing.**'[23] This method is very easy for its people, those chosen to receive the beauty of its gifts. Such a traveller may arrive in a breath and outstrip those who have striven for very long.

'All three groups reach the Goal, but some in a more laborious and prolonged manner than others. The Shaykh who knows how to treat ailments and has expert knowledge of the attributes of the souls and their motives is able to take each group along its particular straight path and cause the 'loser' to change back to 'the best constitution'[01]. This is because human souls are mirrors for Lordly manifestations and the Shaykh must undertake to clear and polish them for each disciple according to the opacity and rust of his mirror.

'Beware of exaggeration and excessive severity, for the Real is nearer to you than your jugular vein.' [End of quotation]

Shaykh Zarrūq[02], may God be pleased with him, composed two tracts in explanation of the Shādhilī method. He called the first *al-Uṣūl* (The Principles) and the other *al-Ummahāt* (The Mothers). In *al-Uṣūl* he says, 'The principles of our path are five: to fear God both in private and in public, to follow the Sunna in both word and deed, to disregard created beings whether they be for or against you, to remain contented with God ﷻ, both in scarcity and in abundance, and to return to God in both ease and hardship.' He explains these five at length, using words not far from those of Ghazālī and others, and then says, 'The bases of this are strength of resolve, preserving what deserves to be preserved, serving with excellence, penetrating willpower, and the magnification of [God's] favors.' He again

01 The best constitution, according to the Qur'ān, is the state of the human spirit before its attachment to the physical form with the resultant appearance of the ego and its ailments and veils. It may also be taken to mean the original nature of Adam and the first generations of mankind who had still not drawn too far away from the Garden.

02 Shaykh Aḥmad al-Zarrūq, a well-known Mālikī scholar and Sufi master of Moroccan origin and author of numerous treatises and commentaries, died at Misurata, Libya, around 899/1493.

explains these at length, and then says, 'The bases of this are the pursuit of knowledge to be able to conform to orders, keeping the company of Shaykhs and brothers with the aim of gaining insight, forsaking concessions and interpretations[01] with the aim of being preserved, structuring time with *awrād* with the aim of achieving presence, and accusing the soul in every matter with the aim of forsaking whims and achieving safety from mistakes.'

He then says, 'The bases of our remedies for ailments are keeping the stomach light in food, taking refuge in God, fleeing every situation which might go wrong, continuous asking for forgiveness together with invoking blessings on the Prophet ﷺ in seclusion and in company, and keeping the company of those who guide to God. . .'

He makes other similar statements in this and the other treatise, *al-Ummahāt*.

It is clear from this that the path of al-Ghazālī and that of al-Shādhilī conform to each other and to other paths, even though the manner of travelling varies with each person. They are all agreed that it is necessary to obey orders, observe prohibitions, and refine one's character. This can only be done by following the Prophet ﷺ and the footsteps of the righteous Predecessors. This in turn can only be done by the great majority of people only through knowledge, works, and striving. **God singles out for His mercy whom He will, and God is the Bestower of immense favor.**[24]

Here ends what I wished to quote from the writings and utterances of earlier scholars, may God reward them on our behalf.

May God's blessings and peace be upon our master Muḥammad, his Family and Companions. Praise belongs to God, Lord of the Worlds.

---

01 Concession (*Rukhṣa*) is the opposite of resolution (*ʿAzīma*). Concession is to pursue the easiest and most reduced option in all acts of worship; resolution is to take the strictest and hardest options in following *Sharīʿa*, so as always to fulfill one's obligations in the most complete manner. 'Interpretation' here means searching for farfetched interpretations for legal texts so as to evade obligations such as *Zakāt* and fasting.

The Four Circles

FATḤ BAṢĀ'IR AL-IKHWĀN

BI-SHARḤ DAWĀ'IR AL-ISLĀM

WA AL-ĪMĀN WA AL-IḤSĀN WA AL-ʿIRFĀN

(INSIGHTS FOR THE BRETHREN ON THE CIRCLES

OF ISLĀM, ĪMĀN, IḤSĀN, AND ʿIRFĀN)

ḤABĪB ʿABD AL-RAḤMĀN

IBN ʿABD ALLĀH BALFAQĪH

Translator's Introduction

Ḥabīb ʿAbd al-Raḥmān Balfaqīh belongs to the generation that followed that of the 'Renewer' of the twelfth century AH, Imām al-Ḥaddād. Born at Tarīm in 1110/1699, he studied under his father Sayyid ʿAbd Allāh ibn Aḥmad Balfaqīh, his maternal grandfather, his uncle, and his elder brother, and then for ten years under Imām ʿAbd Allāh al-Ḥaddād. Later on during his travels he learned from other scholars in Ḥaḍramawt, the Ḥijāz and the Yemen, becoming an expert in the Jurisprudence of all four orthodox schools, the sciences of the Principles of Religion, Qur'ānic commentary, the sciences of *ḥadīth*, those of Arabic, and astronomy. His ability to make effective use of this extensive knowledge by means of his high intelligence and exceptional memory led to Imām al-Ḥaddād calling him *ʿAllāmat al-Dunyā* or the World's Top Scholar.

In addition, Ḥabīb ʿAbd al-Raḥmān was not only a gifted poet but also a very practical and efficient manager of financial resources. He was able to acquire many palm tree plantations, the revenue from which was well spent on building and maintaining seventeen mosques and providing generous hospitality for his numerous guests.

While engaged in these pursuits, he also managed to travel the spiritual path with great efficiency, benefit from his spiritual masters, and receive the Major Opening to become an accomplished Sufi.

Ḥabīb ʿAbd al-Raḥmān died at Tarīm in 1173/1760. His works are still taught in ʿAlawī circles to this day, and his verses are frequently quoted.

In this unique treatise, Ḥabīb ʿAbd al-Raḥmān Balfaqīh discusses the familiar and much commented three levels of *Islām*, *Īmān*, and *Iḥsān* which, together with knowledge of the Signs of the Times, constitute the religion of Islam in all its dimensions.

Islam has been traditionally described in a hierarchical three-tiered manner, based upon a key Tradition of the Prophet ﷺ, in which he defined *Islām, Īmān*, and *Iḥsān*. *Islām* is defined as surrendering to God's will by accepting the Five Pillars, which are the Testimony of Divine Unity and the Prophethood of Muḥammad ﷺ, the Ritual Prayer, *Zakāt*, the Fast of Ramaḍān, and finally the Pilgrimage or *Ḥajj*. In the words of Ḥabīb ʿAbd al-Raḥmān Balfaqīh, '*Islām* comes from *istislām*, surrender, because it is to surrender to God and obey Him in His every command. He who surrenders to God in this manner outwardly and inwardly will be safe from all sins and from retribution, and will reach his ultimate aims in this world and in the Abode of Peace.

Īmān or faith is defined as belief in God, His angels, His Scriptures, His Messengers, the Last Day, and Predestination (*qadar*). Again in the words of Ḥabīb ʿAbd al-Raḥmān Balfaqīh, '*Īmān* is from *amn* and *iṭmiʾnān*, or security and tranquility. He who believes in God, His Attributes and everything He has revealed in the verses of the Qur'an, believes His promises and His threats, and behaves accordingly in every matter, will be safe and satisfied in both this world and the Next and will enjoy God's good pleasure. **Indeed upon God's protégés there will be no fear, nor shall they grieve; those who believed and feared God.**[25]

Iḥsān or excellence is defined as the practice of the first two with sincerity and effectiveness, leading to 'worshiping God as if you were seeing Him, for if you see Him not, He sees you.'

These three levels are seen to correspond to *Sharīʿa*, *Ṭarīqa*, and *Ḥaqīqa*, and the author conceives of them as ever-widening concentric circles but makes a distinction between *Iḥsān*, which means excellence in the application of *Sharīʿa* and *Ṭarīqa*, and *ʿIrfān*, or inward knowledge, the direct knowledge of God which is the result of *Iḥsān* and the ultimate aim of the Path. Most other authors would include *ʿIrfān* or *maʿrifa* in their definition of *Iḥsān*. Here, however, it is placed in a circle of its own; but the author also explains that in reality the number of circles in the gradation is indefinite, with *ʿIrfān* opening up onto the infinite Reality of the One.

The four circles are discussed in the traditional Bā-ʿAlawī style, combining profundity of meaning with concision, bringing out the essentials of a vast subject with a clarity that makes it easy to assimilate, while opening up windows into the spiritual depths that are at the root of every science.

PREFACE

In the Name of God, Most Merciful and Compassionate

All Praise belongs to God, the One, the Bountiful, of immense munificence, who deigns in His grace to lead to *Islām*, *Īmān*, *Iḥsān*, and *ʿIrfān*, and grant guidance and clarification; who has sent Messengers, may His blessings be upon them, with sure knowledge and discernment, keeping for the Chosen One among them, God's blessings and peace be upon him, the summons that comprises all other summons and clarifications for all matters, both outward and inward, from beginning to end[01]. Thus did God render the Way to Himself clear through changing circumstances, and thus did He conclude all religions with this religion, which includes all kinds of lights and right guidance. May His blessings and peace be upon him, his family, who are the stars of guidance, his Companions, who are the lanterns of both outward and inward direct knowledge, and those of his followers who excelled in their adherence to the pattern of his Sunna and the guidance of the Qur'ān. For the Qur'ān is the rope of God, connected to true, continu-

01 The summons that comprises all other summons is that of the Seal of all Prophets ﷺ, which is the final, all-embracing Divine message that comprises everything that all previous Envoys have brought to mankind. The summons that comprises all summons also comprises the five tongues mentioned by Imām al-Ḥaddād: summoning the common people with the tongue of *Sharīʿa* to *Sharīʿa*, the people of *Sharīʿa* with the tongue of *Ṭarīqa* to *Ṭarīqa*, the people of *Ṭarīqa* with the tongue of *Ḥaqīqa* to *Ḥaqīqa*, the people of *Ḥaqīqa* with the tongue of *ḥaqq* to *ḥaqq*, and the people of *ḥaqq* with the tongue of *ḥaqq* to *ḥaqq*.

ally renewed Revelation[01]. It is the explanation of all things and contains, with the clearest evidence, the details of every science, and the principles of every judgment. As for the noble Sunna, it is for the Qur'ān the most complete explanation and clarification.

By the Qur'ān, the Muḥammadan Sunna which expounds it, and their understanding by the scholars and their using them to guide to Him, God has absolved this Aḥmadan[02] community from the need for further Messengers or Revelations. His Aḥmadan religion and Muḥammadan pattern[03] remain clear, pure, and unblemished for whoever has knowledge and faith. There is no slackening, no misleading, no ambiguity, nothing problematic, no weakness and no imbalance for those with inward knowledge and certitude.

The Qur'ān and its religion remain fresh, for God, in His grace, raises in each century those who renew it by clarifying the evidence and strengthen-

01 The expression 'continually renewed Revelation' refers to the ever-renewed opening of new meanings in the hearts and minds of scholars and saints reflecting on the Qur'ān, so that new insights are produced by each generation and will continue to be until the end of time. The Qur'ān, being the uncreated Word of God, is by definition infinite and will continue to offer new aspects of meaning in this world and yet more in the Next.

02 Aḥmad is the Prophet's name in Heaven, which is where Revelation originates. It is thus the name by which he is known to previous Prophets and mentioned in their Scriptures; Muḥammad is his name on earth, where he made his physical appearance, where Revelation was received and transmitted, and where each of his utterances, actions, and approvals becomes a Sunna. Muslims are called the Muḥammadan Community and also the Aḥmadan Community. The latter is based on the precedent when Moses asked his Lord about a certain Community, yet to come, the description of which God had given him in the Tablets, and was told, 'They are the Community of Aḥmad.' Abū Nuʿaym, *Ḥilyat al-awliyā'*, 5:384; Al-Ḥakīm al-Tirmidhī, *Nawādir al-uṣūl*, 1:355.

03 The Qur'ān says, **The Religion in God's sight is Islam.** [3:19] Archetypal Religion in God's sight in the higher worlds is Islam, which means total surrender to God's will. This archetypal religion manifests itself on earth in various forms according to time and place, each form receiving a name to differentiate it from the others, but ultimately their reality is one. All previous true religion, as combined before in Abraham, peace be upon him, before diverging to be gathered again in Islam, is called before the appearance of the Prophet ﷺ, the Aḥmadan religion. As for the Muḥammadan pattern, it is the *Sunna* that was seen and heard after the appearance of the Prophet ﷺ, and constitutes the practice of Muslims today.

ing the arguments[01]. They summon to God, clear-sightedly[02], as concerns *Sharīʿa, Ṭarīqa and Ḥaqīqa*, in the circles of *Islām* and *Īmān*, knowledge and clarification, and *Iḥsān* and *ʿIrfān*.

To proceed: A brother, a man of God who is attached to us for the love of God, in accordance with the dictates of faith on the path of excellence, has asked me and insisted that I write for him a comprehensive counsel of clarification, that it may become for him a beneficial provider of insight and reminder in matters of religion. He requested that it embrace the beginning and end and be complete outwardly and inwardly, in such a way as to unite the teachings of both the pious scholars and the Knower by God saints. He asked me of my knowledge on the subject, as well as what I have personally experienced, fathomed, and tried in the way of knowledge and certitude. I say, then, and all success and guidance are by God:

Know that this matter has a beginning and an end, a first and a last, an outward and an inward, principles and applications, and totality and parts.

- Its ultimate goal is reached only when its guidance is made straight.
- Its end can only be reached if its beginning is sound.
- Its first becomes perfect only by its last.
- Its inward can be reached only through its outward.
- There is no way to its applications (branches) save through its principles.
- There is no realization of its totality save by knowledge of its parts[03].

---

01 A reference to the *ḥadīth* that states, *God shall raise with every century those who renew for this nation their religion.* [Abū Dāwūd, *Sunan*, 4291]. The wording of the *ḥadīth* does not permit a firm conclusion as to whether the renewing function would be assumed by one or more persons each century and scholarly opinions concerning this have diverged. The function of the Renewer is to address each century in the language and with the arguments best suited for it, and to solve the problems peculiar to that time. It is reasonable to assume that for practical reasons there would be a Renewer for each geographical region, as well as for each of the levels of *Islām, Imān* and *Iḥsān*, which does not preclude that all these different parts of the one function be united in one person, as they will undoubtedly be in the Mahdī.

02 A reference to Qur'ān [12:108] **Say, 'This is my way. I summon to God, clear-sightedly, I and those who follow me.'**

03 The ultimate goal is to enter the presence of God. Choosing a path that is not a strict and insightful application of the teachings of the Qur'ān and Sunna would obviously make it impossible to reach the goal. This is why a strong foundation based on a wholeheartedly sincere application of the Sacred Law is necessary, since only a

The whole is a single religion and a straight path which has stations, drinking-places, degrees and ranks. **All shall have their degrees, according to what they wrought**[26]. **God will raise up in rank those of you who have believed and been given knowledge**[27].

Since knowledge of the Book and Sunna is a unified whole, to be able to conform to the applications and parts necessitates accepting the principles and totality. To belie a part is to belie the whole.

The people of each degree take from each verse of the Qur'ān and each act of obedience as much as is appropriate to their degree. Each drinks from his own source, according to his aptitude, the receptivity of his heart, his faith, devotion, and nearness. For each verse of the Qur'ān, *ḥadīth*, act of obedience, of remembrance, or of worship has an outward and an inward, a limit and a place of ascent, and this indefinitely.[01] Each seeker takes his share from each of those desirable things, according to what has been providentially allotted to him and the profundity of his understanding and knowledge.

---

sound beginning may lead to a sound end. Since the process is likened to a tree, the seed that contains the traveler's path in potential, here called the 'first', only attains its perfection or completion when the purpose of it which is the attainment of the final goal is reached, which is here called the 'last'. Again, the goal which is inward can only be reached by the practice of the outward aspects of the Sacred Law, which is outward. The application of various details concerning the path and the difference in requirements between various types of travelers are governed by knowledge of the principles, which is what is properly called 'wisdom'. The totality in question is the whole that is more than the sum of its parts, and it is only by knowledge of the various parts and using the principles of wisdom to connect these parts and understand the relationship between them that the 'synthesis' can be reached.

01 A *ḥadīth* states that each verse of the Qur'ān possesses an outward and an inward, a limit and a 'place of ascent'. The *ḥadīth* has a weak chain of transmission but is nevertheless accepted by Sufis who know its truth by contemplative verification, although the majority of them have always refrained from explaining it. Here the author extends the concept to include not only Qur'ān, but *ḥadīths*, acts of worship, *dhikr*, and all other acts of obedience. Each of those should be understood to have an outward form, which has to be performed properly, and an inward dimension, which is sincerity and concentration. The limit is what separates one entity from another, but more importantly the place one has to reach to see what lies beyond it. Once one is aware that beyond the limit he has reached are other things to seek, he searches for the place of ascent that will allow him to rise and reach them. There he will find yet another limit and another place of ascent, and so on indefinitely.

Take for example, the Word of Sincerity,[01] which is the Principle of Principles.

When the people of *Īmān* say *Lā ilāha illā Allāh*, they mean, 'None is to be worshiped save God.' When on the road of *Iḥsān*, they will mean, 'There is none to be sought save God.' Once they have realized *ʿIrfān*, they will mean, 'There is none that exists save God.'

Again, with the *Basmala* which initiates every situation, they will say *Bism Allāh*, meaning by that their attachment (to God) or *taʿalluq*. At the second level they will intend emulating the Divine Attributes or *takhalluq*. At the third level they will intend realization or *taḥaqquq*.[02]

Thus the people of each level take their share from these two Words, these two noble invocations, and drink of their beverages, according to the differences and variations between them, which are endless within each level.

For instance, at the first level, as concerns acts of worship and attachment, the [spiritual gifts brought about by these are] both general and special. They vary in kind according to how each was brought on, each thing allotted, depending on its limits.[03] You may apply this to the rest.

Know that when in His generosity God, Transcendent and Exalted is He, sent His Messenger, our Master Muḥammad ﷺ, He gave him 'comprehensiveness of speech'[04], made his religion easy, eased its transmission

---

01 The Word of Sincerity is *Lā ilāha illā A'llāh*. It is also called the Word of Unification, the Phrase of the Testimony, of Sincerity, Reality, Truth, the Pledge, Faith, Piety, the Good Word, the Abiding Word, God's Most Exalted Word, the Word of Intercession, the Price of the Garden, and the Key to the Garden. (Ḥabīb Aḥmad Mashhūr al-Ḥaddād, *Key to the Garden*, Chicago, 2003, p. 4)

02 Acquiring the Divine Attributes, as enjoined by the Prophet ﷺ, requires effort and perseverance. One trains oneself to be generous, patient, forbearing, and so on. Realization is to witness these attributes in action in creation with the Eye of the Heart, to see that it is by the Name of God that everything exists, moves, halts, reacts, and so on.

03 The first level is that of faith and attachment to God, together with the practice of the acts of worship prescribed by the Sacred Law. These will attract Divine gifts that are general, shared by all believers, such as forgiveness of sins, increase in faith and certainty, insight into religious matters, and increase in determination and sincerity, according to the kind of act and depth of attachment. Then there are the special gifts bestowed on special people each according to his receptivity and qualification. These will consist in unveilings and the contemplative knowledge of Divine secrets.

04 The Prophet, God's blessings and peace be upon him, said, *I have been granted com-*

to the people through him, and relieved his Community of their burden and of all difficulties by his *baraka*. And He summed up the entire religion in the words of the Testimony (*Shahāda*), which is the beginning of the circles of *Islām* and *Īmān*, then deployed it in larger circles endlessly, to suit the degrees of the pious and the levels of religion, up to the highest level which is that of the Prophets and Messengers.

Uttering the two Testimonies ushers one into *Islām*. This is the point around which revolve the circle including *Islām* and *Īmān*, then that of knowledge and the clarification of it, followed by that of *Iḥsān* and *'Irfān*, and so on endlessly.

Let us clarify this matter in four circles, with God's help.

The first circle is the circle of *Islām* and *Īmān*, which is to learn the principles and applications in a global synthetic manner, with conviction, conformity and submission.

The second circle is that of fathoming the principles to their roots and delving into the details of each part and each application. It is that of broadening and clarifying one's knowledge.

The third circle is that of moving from the outward to the inward and from knowledge and logical proof to experience and feeling. This is the way of *Iḥsān*.

The fourth circle is last in relation to those before it, but first in relation to those that come after. This is the contemplation of reality and the knowledge of the limits and places of ascent for every outward and inward thing in the path of inward knowledge.

FIRST CIRCLE

Know that to enter *Islām* and *Īmān* one has to utter the two Testimonies, know their meaning, abide by their rules, and submit to their dictates outwardly and inwardly. By this alone can *Islām* be achieved and *Īmān*

---

prehensiveness of speech. [Bukhārī, *Ṣaḥīḥ*, 2977] This means that he was able to express a richness of meanings succinctly, yet with clarity. The most synthetic speech is that of the Qur'ān, followed by that of the Prophet ﷺ. Both possess many dimensions of meaning and stand clearly apart from the utterances of sages and scholars.

completed. Whoever dies in this state dies in his sound original nature, the *fiṭra*[01], and his religion is complete.

The explanation of this is that the two Testimonies comprise in sum all of religion. As for beliefs, the fact is clear from their wording. As for the rest, it is because one has to submit to their implications as concerns rulings and actions, then one has to intend to perpetuate this submission at all times and in all situations. This all-inclusive resolution stands in for repeated individual intentions, for there is no end to them. This is why the resolution to conform to all of them stands in for the actual performance [of those acts that one is unable to], since there is no end to acts [of obedience]. Thus does one become aware that acts have been prescribed to strengthen religion, expand the meaning of the two testimonies, and increase certitude.

Remembrance (*dhikr*) was prescribed to remind and purify the heart from being distracted by others; its effect is thus profitable to him who remembers, not the Remembered, and its beneficial consequences go to the servant in every way.

Uttering the two Testimonies is to what follows it what a date-stone is to the palm-tree which grows from it. The root of the palm and its branches spread out according to the goodness of the soil and sweetness of the water.

When the tree of religion is planted by sowing the seed in a good heart, watering it with the water of good works that reaches the heart by attentiveness, guided by knowledge from a pure source, at the hands of the Near Angels, with the inward assistance of the saints, while keeping the company of the virtuous, then the eye of certitude opens to the meaning of religion and is accorded every kind of light and every act of the pious. The heart lives therefrom the goodly life, in joy and happiness, and dies not with the death of the body, but remains evermore in felicity and bliss.

But when planted in a corrupt wicked heart, watered with the bitter water of sins and depravity, it will not survive, but in its place will grow the tree of confusion and manifest error, at the hands of the accursed Devil. Religion then dies and so does the heart, even before the death of the body. The person then remains in the darkness of remoteness, expulsion, and misery ever after. The whole matter belongs to God, Lord of all beings.

---

01 The *fiṭra* is the original nature of mankind, the nature of Adam ﷺ, who was a Prophet and thus a perfect human being. The original nature of mankind is perfection. Islam, being *Dīn al-Fiṭra*, strives to raise Muslims to that level of perfection.

As stated earlier, the central point of the circle of *Islām* is the utterance of the two Testimonies. This circle continues to expand under the impulse of the details within this sum, the performance of the prescribed rules and acts, the clarification of one's beliefs through sound reflection, and the understanding of logical proof.

Thus, in accordance with the meanings contained in the two Testimonies and deployed in the details of religion, *Islām* and *Īmān* will increase, which means submission to God and returning to Him, by knowledge and by action, at all times and in every circumstance. He who finds that his good works neither increase his faith nor strengthen his certitude, let him know that this is because his works are defective and his effort is meager, owing to lack of sincerity and truthfulness in his intention; or it may be due to an ailment in his heart that has corrupted it so as to spoil his works. Examples of these ailments are complacency, contentment, and admiration for one's own works, or observing others and becoming attached to them and anxious to look good in their eyes. This leads to ostentation, arrogance, jealousy, deceit, and rancor. It also leads to strengthening the 'soul that incites to evil' so that it gains supremacy over the heart by the power of its appetites, which results in hardness of the heart, lack of fear, and immersion in sins. Another ailment is to be inwardly vile and under the Devil's sway, subject to his insinuations and deceptions.

Let the servant who has been granted guidance strive to purify his heart of all these major causes of ruin and cleanse it from these blemishes and destructive ailments. Let him exert his utmost effort to remedy his heart, improve, purify, guide, and lead it to success. For when the heart is good, the body and all other things are good, but when the heart is ruined, so is everything else. This is why the ailments of the heart are more worthy of being attended to than those of the body in general or any one organ in particular. One wonders greatly at him who, when his hand or foot suffer an illness, exerts himself in every possible way to have it treated, yet when it is his heart that is unwell and his mind that is ill, has no thoughts of treating them and neglects them until his heart dies of a death after which it can never come to life again. The heart is then sealed, his religion is lost, and he remains a failure forever. **No! But what they earned has rusted upon their hearts. No! But upon that day they shall be veiled from their Lord.**[28] **Those who forgot God, so He caused them to forget themselves, those are the corrupt.**[29] **So for breaking their pact We cursed them and made their**

hearts hard.[30] **But God sealed them up for their disbelief, so they believe not except a few.**[31]

How can one endowed with reason forget his intelligence and his heart, the only things that distinguish him from animals, or his religion, the only thing that makes him better than the disbelievers? **So let not the life of this world deceive you, and let not the deceiver deceive you concerning God.**[32] **Every soul shall taste of death. You shall surely be paid in full your wages on Resurrection Day. Whoever is removed from the Fire and admitted to the Garden shall have succeeded. The life of this world is but the comfort of illusion.**[33] How can he whom God has blessed with reason and invited to wisdom and success contentedly neglect his final end and remain indifferent to whether his heart is good or corrupt? How can he expend the invaluable seconds of his lifetime in bestial appetites such as eating, drinking and mating, and remain contented with resembling cattle in his comings and goings? In reality, he is even more astray than cattle, for he carries the burden of sin and evil-doing.

Let every human being consider what makes him human, what raises him from the pits of defectiveness to the pinnacles of loftiness and excellence. This is nothing but reason, religion, and a heart filled with light and certitude.

Are they equal, those who know and those who know not?[34] **Is he who is a believer like him who is corrupt? They are not equal.**[35] **Or do those who commit evil deeds think that We shall make them as those who believe and do good works, the same in their life and death? How ill they judge!**[36] **Is he who was dead and to whom We gave him life and set for him a light to walk by among people as one whose likeness is that he is in the shadows, from which he will never come out? Thus was their conduct made to seem fair in the eyes of the disbelievers.**[37]

How many a human being is not really human! A human being only in outward form, but in reality a serpent, a beast of prey, a dog, or a devil, since it is the attributes of these that are dominant in him and it is their book that he reads. Therefore, be not deceived by his appearance, for only his reality is important. This reality only becomes outwardly visible in the World to Come.

He for whom God wishes goodness and success, He will purify his heart and body from sins and all kinds of ruinous filth and He will make easy for him the constant remembrance of Him and perseverance in acts of obedience. Then He will show him that He is the One to whom he is constantly indebted for the favor of creation and for those of continuing existence, sustenance, and safety from perils, for it is He and no other who gave him what he has, guided him to it, and inspired him to his acts of obedience. **Had God not guided us, we had surely never been guided.**[38] **They regard it as a favor to you they embraced Islam! Say: 'Regard not your Islam as a favor to me; no, but rather God conferred a favor upon you, in that He guided you to faith, if it be that you are truthful.'**[39] **But God has endeared faith to you and embellished it in your hearts; and He has made detestable to you disbelief, corruption and disobedience. Those are the right-minded, by God's favor and grace.**[40] The signs of a goodly heart are satisfaction with right guidance and faith, detestation of disbelief, corruption and transgression, the love of goodness and good people, and benefiting from one's remembrance, reminding from others, and the recitation of the Qur'ān. **And remind, for reminding profits believers.**[41] **He will be reminded who fears.**[42] **And when His Signs are recited to them, it increases them in faith, and they put their trust in their Lord.**[43] **As for those who believe, it increases their faith and they rejoice.**[44] **God has sent down the fairest discourse as a Book consistent with itself, paired. It makes the skins shiver of those who fear their Lord, then their skins and their hearts soften to the remembrance of God.**[45]

He who neither profits from remembrance and the Qur'ān, nor becomes humble at reminding and explanations, his faith is weak and his heart sick, for it has been covered over with '**that which covers**'[01]. Let him make up for what has elapsed of his lifetime and what he has neglected therein of his duty. Let him exert himself in being true and sincere with God, let him purify and liberate his heart from vile things, keep to the remembrance of God and remain constantly absorbed in it, take every opportunity for good works, maintaining vigilance with God and presence in every state and situation. The heart will then fill with certitude and he will ascend the steps of submission to God in *Islām*, finding in it reassurance as he travels the road of *Īmān*, to the ladder of *Iḥsān*, and ever-rising stations of *'Irfān*.

---

01 '**That which covers**' is the expression used in the Qur'ān to indicate the ailments of the heart and various veils separating it from the perception of the truth. These are described as 'rust' over the heart in a *ḥadīth* which adds that the rust is removed by the constant remembrance of God.

He will then see the truth as such, as if with his eyesight. **For such as this let those who work do so.**[46] Good works are gifts from God to His servant and favors from God bestowed upon him, for which He will later reward him. He causes them to be the attribute of those He wishes to draw nearer, and a manifest sign. He also made them the key to His acceptance and the door to His satisfaction and to felicity in the Gardens. The door is never opened for him who turns away from good works, whereas he who performs them is knocking on the door of Generosity and placing himself in a position to receive the donations of the Beneficent, the Bestowing.

He who is entirely absorbed in the worship of his Lord and immersed in His remembrance still remains incapable of giving Him His due of thankfulness, for acts of worship are themselves nothing but more favors, greater than the greatest favors. For it is He who has led him to obedience to Him and made him of those who enter His presence; this is the greatest of favors and gifts and the highest of degrees, the worth of which he will remain unable to grasp or thank for, however much he may strive and exert himself to be thankful, for his intention to be thankful is yet another favor, and so on. Transcendent is He whose favors can only be thanked through His favor, obedience to whom is only possible by His assistance and grace. There is thus no way to thank Him save by awareness of one's incapacity in this respect, confessing to it, and feeling destitute. There is no way to obey Him save by abasement, submission and neediness. As for works, God's favor is evident in them and constant incapacity to thank for them is a perpetual state. Consequently, he who is engaged in rendering thanks, remembering, fasting, and keeping night vigils is more fearful of God than others, because the favors that God bestows upon him are immense, yet he knows he can only remain ever unthankful and neglectful [in comparison to the thanks that are rightfully due to God]. Once you know this, you know that [even] he whose works are perfect may be wary of them, anxious not to see them as his or depend on them, for he sees the favor of God upon him and his deficient thankfulness. How, then, can he depend on them? Good works are not required for themselves, but solely to witness the favor of God, follow the path, obey commands, and because He, Transcendent is He, has made them the door to His proximity and the key to His love. God it is who grants success.

SECOND CIRCLE

This is concerned with establishing the principles in depth, studying the branches and applications in detail, and broadening and clarifying one's knowledge.

Know that in this religion both knowledge and action are necessary, and this from beginning to end, for both its aspects, outward and inward.

Knowledge, even though some of it is merely a tool, is the principle and guide. It is to the believer his minister and intimate friend, and is the method and road leading to every good in this world and the next. It is the best act of worship for he who intends it purely for the sake of God and is sincere in it with Him; for God can never be worshiped with anything better than the comprehension of religion. A single scholar is harder on the Devil than a thousand worshippers.[47] The superiority of a learned man over a [common] worshiper is as that of the Prophet ﷺ over everyone else[01]. He who acquires knowledge and uses it in the *taqwā* of God has attained to the most honorable of the stations of merit and good fortune. He for whom God wishes goodness, He gives him the understanding of religion[48]. The best among you in the Days of Ignorance will remain the best in Islam, on condition that they come to understand[49].

It is therefore incumbent upon every believer to strive to acquire that knowledge by which he will know his religion and strengthen his certitude. He must study the principles and know them as principles, and study the parts and applications in detail, so that this may become his guide to his Lord, to knowledge of Him, and to His satisfaction and nearness. He should acquire an adequate share of each science of religion, whether obligatory or *Sunna*, under a teacher of good counsel, according to the time available and the ability to grasp opportunities. These sciences are those of doctrine, Jurisprudence, Sufism, the sciences of the Qur'ān, those of the *Sunna*, and their ancillaries. He should intend that this be purely for the sake of God, to seek His nearness, for of all the aspects of religion and means of nearness to the Lord of the Worlds, knowledge is the greatest. By this does the servant know himself in his incapacity, deficiency, abasement and poverty, and His Lord in His Immensity, His Independence of him, and the favors

01 The Prophet—may God's blessings and peace be upon him—said, *The superiority of a scholar over a [normal] worshiper is as my superiority over the least amongst you.* [Tirmidhī, *Sunan*, 2685]

He bestows upon him in everything that concerns him. Knowledge that does not produce this result and does not increase this awareness can never be one of the sciences of religion; it is but idle chatter. If it does not yield guidance, light, and certitude, it is but affliction, sterility, and the attribute of the hypocrites. Knowledge that does not draw one nearer to God is unrelated to Him. Knowledge that cuts one off from God or prevents one from remembering Him is more worthy of being called ignorance. Knowledge that causes distraction from God, leading to hardness of the heart, and engaging in prattle, arguments and controversy, is always blameworthy. How many have perished through this, gaining only sins and reproaches! We ask God for protection against deviation from previous rectitude, or abandoning the light for darkness.

He who increases in knowledge but does not increase in humility, neediness toward God and fear of Him, increases only in ignorance. If knowledge does not profit its possessor, ignorance would be more likely to profit him. The same goes for works. Both are but means to attain servitude and humility before God in every situation. We ask God to protect us from knowledge that is of no benefit and works that are not accepted!

A student should attend to the eye of his heart and to that which will cause his religion to thrive and increase the strength of his certitude and his nearness to his Lord. He should guard his soul during the acquisition of knowledge, as much as his rank and understanding allow. We have said before that God in His grace, Transcendent is He, incorporated in the two Testimonies all of religion, so as to make entry into the latter the easiest thing for beginners. Then He explained their meaning in some verses in The Manifest Remembrance,[01] such as *Āyat al-Kursī* and the last two verses of *Sūrat al-Baqara*. Then He explained these verses by the entire Formidable Qur'ān, made the Muḥammadan Sunna a further explanation and clarification, then made the discourses of the scholars an explanation of the Sunna. This process goes on indefinitely. That is the origin and basis of the knowledge of the scholars and the wisdom of the sages, each according to his state and power of expression. In this they are the heirs of the Messengers[02], and God has raised some Messengers above others[03].

01 The Manifest or Explicit Remembrance is the Qur'ān.

02 *Scholars are heirs to the Prophets*, says a *ḥadīth*. [Tirmidhī, *Sunan*, 2682]

03 According to the Qur'ān, Divine Messengers are of various ranks, the implication

Some of them He spoke to and some He raised in rank even though they were late in appearing [on earth]. The same applies to the scholars, for God gives wisdom to whomsoever He wishes, whenever He wishes, in the way He wishes. The favor of God upon this Community is like abundant rain. How much have the ancestors left for the latecomers[01]!

Let not the student think that he could ever achieve mastery in all the sciences, even were he to study for a thousand years. It is more appropriate for him to take the best of each art and what is necessary. He will need doctrinal knowledge, for he is under obligation to know what is necessarily true concerning God and His Messenger, what is possible and what is impossible. This is the first of obligations and the origin of all acts of worship. He should then move on from sum to details and from beginning to completion. In this way he will have acquired the knowledge of God in the common sense[02], which is that upon which religion and Islam rest. He should move from this principle to the special meaning which is a light in the heart that God casts into the hearts of those whom He chooses of the élite. Let him beware strongly of delving into theology (*kalām*)[03], since it may lead to confusion and doubts; for he may grasp the doubting statement but not the answer, and [satanic] insinuations and [figments of his] imagination may intervene, which may lead him so far as to stray out of the circle of Islam. This is why many eminent scholars have pronounced it *ḥarām*. In this it resembles many of the sciences of the ancients, whether People of the Book or otherwise, and the discourses of the latecomers on

---

being that their heirs, the scholars, are similarly of varying ranks.

01 This means that early scholars have not exhausted the knowledge of the Qur'ān and Sunna; there is therefore still much to do for the latecomers.

02 This refers to mental knowledge, that of the mind, but that of the heart remains yet to be acquired.

03 The science of *Kalām* is mainly concerned with the beliefs of Muslims as concerns Divine Attributes. It evolved in response to the need to answer heretical thinkers producing deviant interpretations of the Book and *Sunna*. It ended up being made of interminable arguments, stating one heretical belief after another, then answering every possible variation in exhausting details. It flourished early during the Abbasid caliphate when most heretical sects made their appearance, but has nowadays lost its appeal, especially since it has frequently been denigrated by realized scholars and Sufis. However, its dependence upon the rigorous rules of logic makes it an essential component in the training of scholars.

essential realities and subtleties[01]. Despite these containing many sciences and profitable information, it is difficult to disentangle them safely and escape being waylaid by their twists, except for the rare man of genius, master of both outward and inward knowledge; it is only for such a man that such a course is permissible.

As for *fiqh*, he needs it to know what is obligatory for him in the way of ritual prayer, *Zakāt*, fasts, *Ḥajj*, and other things. It is necessary for the soundness of his religion, and to be able to distinguish the obligatory from the supererogatory. There is no harm in studying it in detail and in depth, to know how to judge each action and situation and distinguish *ḥalāl* from *ḥarām*. The student of *fiqh* cannot be subject to reproach unless he studies merely for the acquisition of eminence and wealth, or indulges in circumstantial discussions, controversy, or arguments, or is distracted from the remembrance of God and the Last Abode by preoccupation with abstruse details, for this may lead to hardness of the heart and he may thus miss what is more important in the way of obligatory or recommended acts. He whose study of *fiqh* leads to this will have fallen into the very thing he is trying to escape. But he who studies it by God, sees in it a reminder of God, remembers God abundantly during his studies, safeguards himself against its problems, disputes and arguments, and intends it to be solely for the sake of God, for him it becomes the best of all acts of obedience and the worthiest thing in which to expend his valuable time. It becomes a remembrance of God, for to remember God's prescriptions is to remember God. We find in the verses of the Book of God mention being made of commercial transactions, marriage, divorce, and other rulings. These are all recited during the ritual prayer and thus become prayer, for their origin is the remembrance of God and they lead back to presence with Him; and presence with God is that which inevitably brings on nearness, while distraction from God is the cause of remoteness, even if one be preoccupied with one of the major matters of religion. Take for example loyalty to parents: most people serve them without forming a true intention, for habit here dominates over worship and there is no presence with God. Hence it is rare to see its effect appear on them and it becoming the cause

01 The reference is to the works of such Sufis as Ibn al-ʿArabī and al-Jīlī, who disclose things which most other Sufis prefer to leave undisclosed.

of their success, as once happened to Uways al-Qaranī, the Master of the Followers[01]. Success is from God.

As for Sufism, one needs it to know what is incumbent upon him in the way of sincerity and freeing one's works from flaws, self-admiration caused by what he has been given of works and gifts, and purifying one's heart from vile things by treading the path of the élite. This is how works become unblemished and hearts clear and prepared to receive the experience of the knowledge of God ﷻ and behold the Unseen. It is without doubt that which comprises all that is best in religion, the place of ascent of the works of the pious, the fountain where the beverage of direct knowledge and the wine of certitude are drunk. He who has tasted none of it and acquired none of its attributes remains a loser, even if he should acquire all the knowledge of both the ancients and the latecomers. However, because it is well hidden, it is rarely found, and because it is so precious, it is rarely attained. How many who have claimed to possess it are unworthy of it; and how many have been deceived because of their pride and ignorance! It is attained by effort, and then only by rare exceptional individuals, under the tutorship of a perfect skillful master. The gifts of God, however, never cease to descend on His people and the donations of His generosity are ever raining on those who keep their company, sit with them, and love them. To peruse their books and to talk about their states and merits are well-tried remedies for the heart's ailments and for sound repentance and the forgiveness of sins. To sit in their company and increase their numbers, to be guided by their lights and emulate their conduct, when accompanied by sincerity toward them and the confession of one's defective attributes and evil actions, are the key to the Opening[02] and the contemplation of the Unseen. They are

---

01 Uways al-Qaranī was contemporary with the Prophet, may God's blessings and peace be upon him, but never saw him because he lived in Yemen and had a sick mother whom he felt obliged to serve. He received the inward influx of light from the Blessed Prophet at a distance, thus becoming a great saint and the Master of the Followers, the best that is of those who followed after the Companions. The Prophet, God's blessings and peace be upon him, told two of his foremost Companions and eventual successors, ʿUmar and ʿAlī, that Uways would some day come in a caravan from Yemen and that they were to look for him and ask him to pray for them, which they did.

02 The Opening (*al-Fatḥ*) is the rending of the veil covering the heart so that it comes to behold what is invisible to most human beings. It is of many degrees, beginning with true dream visions, then the vision of the subtle forms of the Intermediary

'the people whose companions never suffer wretchedness'[01]. Those who love them catch up with them, and none who is with them will ever be deprived. He has been granted providential success who keeps to their doorsteps, expecting the favor of the Bestower by knocking on the door to good works and drawing nearer, but without paying attention to either his knowledge or his works, for that is the greatest veil. He will never achieve complete servitude to God so long as there remains in him anything belonging to other than Him. Nor will he ever take a clear draught of Sufism until he forsakes his ego and abandons attributing praiseworthy qualities to himself, or finding comfort in other company than God's. This is a door that can be knocked upon only by poverty and neediness, and opened only by the relentless pursuit of that knowledge which draws one nearer to God and by constant remembrance. None enters but he who is free from self, claims, power, or ability under all circumstances. Flee therefore to God, flee![02] How near is the road for the sincere! Together with sincerity in striving there needs to be assistance from God. Together with effort there needs to be opening from God. **Those who strive in Us, We shall assuredly guide them to Our ways; and God is indeed with those who excel.**[50] The Pourer[03] is everlasting, and none despairs of the generosity of God or loses hope in His mercy but the disbelievers. How often do Divine gifts draw the remote servant nearer! How often does the hand of Divine solicitude save deviant and sinful people and raise them above others whose attributes are noble and ranks eminent! Only he who is himself deprived denies the favors of God and His generosity towards His servants, and antagonizes His saints and His people[04]. This happens to those who are overcome with jealousy,

---

Worlds, then that of the Divine Acts and Attributes. The word *fatḥ* also means 'victory'. *Al-Fatḥ al-Kabīr*, the Greater Opening, unveils all the degrees of universal existence.

01 A reference to the well-known *ḥadīth* which describes the circles of remembrance and declares that those who join the people of remembrance, even if they do not belong to them, never suffer wretchedness. See p. 27 footnote 02. 'Wretchedness' here means punishment in Hell, whether for Muslim sinners or for disbelievers. [Bukhārī, *Ṣaḥīḥ*, 6408; Muslim, *Ṣaḥīḥ*, 4854]

02 **Flee to God!** commands the Qur'ān. [50:51]

03 The Pourer is He who pours the beverage of the spirits into the cups of the sanctified hearts. He is the Giver, the Eternal, and His gifts of lights and inward knowledge are ever being renewed to His lovers.

04 God is the One who grants success. He gives it and He withholds it. Those from

wronging themselves. They remain in misery and unhappiness until they destroy themselves by their wrongdoing. In reality, they are the ones who are wronged, for the objects of their jealousy remain unharmed. On the contrary, God increases them in favors and completes His generosity towards them. This is no different from the God's way with previous Prophets, with saints and with the People[01].

As for the sciences of the Qur'ān and Sunna, they are the bases and roots of all sciences, their principles, and the way to master them and understand them in detail. They are necessary if one is to know the source of each piece of information. One also needs to know the merits of their experts and their differences in understanding the explicit and the implicit, and to act according to sound faith and unequivocal Qur'ānic texts and follow those who are well versed in textual evidence and logical proof. Breasts are dilated and lights received when one does the following: [i] reads the Book of God and comprehend its manner of expression; [ii] reads the Traditions of the Messenger of God ﷺ, and learn their meanings; and [iii] studies the lives of the Companions and Followers, then of those who conveyed the Messenger's religion and were his supporters, for these are the virtuous and at the mention of them mercy and peace descend and one becomes clearly connected. As for the ancillary [branches of knowledge], one should learn the Arabic language in detail, which is required to understand the Word of God and that of His Messenger. This is how one remains safe from misconstruing or altering the meaning, or using it out of context. No praise can ever do justice to such a means by which the one granted providential success reaches his goal. In sum, all those branches of knowledge that serve religion are part of religion and are counted among the best acts of obedience to the Lord of the Worlds.

He whose understanding is acute and to whom knowledge comes easily, let him devote all his time to it, save that time which he necessarily has to devote to obligatory and recommended acts, fulfilling the rights of others upon him, and those things that cannot be omitted such as a *ḥizb* of the Qur'ān[02], the *awrād* of the Prophet ﷺ which are prescribed for

---

whom He withholds it are those whose nature is set against light and all that relates to it. These are the 'deprived'.

01 The Sufis.

02 A *ḥizb* is a specified division of the Qur'ān to be recited every day. The Qur'ān's division into thirty *juz'* (portions) is agreed upon everywhere in the Islamic world.

specific situations and times, and supererogatory devotions, whether ritual prayers or otherwise. For these complement the obligatory devotions and were recommended by the Legislator and assigned to particular causes and times. Although the general superiority of knowledge over everything else is well established, the aforementioned things are recommended, subject to their specific conditions.

The merits of knowledge are only obtained by sincerity, truthfulness with God, remembering God by and in it, and not allowing it to distract one from God. We have said before that to remember the prescriptions of God is part of remembering Him, and warned that to be distracted by it from Him by indulging in idle prattling, excessive questioning, controversy, or argument, leads to inattentiveness, then hardness, then death of the heart and loss of concentration, which in turn leads to error and confusion. [We have also warned against] exceeding the limits when studying so that other good works are neglected, whether these be timed obligatory or strongly recommended supererogatory acts, or what should be done along with them. The neglect and loss of these leads to diminution in religion and disobedience of the Lord of the Worlds. What good is there in knowledge that leads to diminution and takes one into disobedience? He who allows himself to neglect his strongly recommended supererogatory acts of worship will inevitably allow neglect eventually to reach his obligatory acts. He who has no *wird* of Prophetic invocations and the litanies of the Sufi masters cannot have a *wārid*[01]. He who turns away from the remembrance of God and regular daily recitations of the Qur'ān and forgets God will be caused to forget himself and the Devil will become his constant companion. He will live in perplexity and arrive blind on Resurrection Day. The [daily] *ḥizb* of Qur'ān is a strongly recommended duty. It is incumbent upon each reciter to preserve what he has learned by heart, for it is easily lost, and to forget a *sūra* or even a verse is one of the greatest sins. It is the vessel of religion, the origin of every light, guidance, knowledge and clarification. Let none be deceived by what he hears of the merits of knowledge and pursue it to

Each *juz'* is further divided into two *ḥizb*s, each of which is then divided into four *rubʿ* or quarters. These *ḥizb*s are different from the *ḥizb* used locally in Ḥaḍramawt, which is one quarter of a *rubʿ*.

01 The *wārid* is the possible Divine response to the *wird*. It takes whatever form the Giver pleases, which may be a major or minor spiritual opening or realization.

the detriment of these obligations and works, for these are necessary for the soundness of the heart and the preservation of faith.

As for him whose understanding is slow, let him spend most of his time in worshipping activities or any other thing attracting Divine reward, whether this be something of benefit to the Muslims or service to the people of religion, or even working for either the obligatory or a recommended means of livelihood.

Let the man of reason make the best of the priceless jewel which is his life, for one instant of it is worth far more than a thousand pearls. He who does not occupy his time with good works and restrain himself **with those who call upon their Lord at morning and evening desiring His Countenance**[51], his ego will occupy him with evil and his life will be spent in vain. He will put off things until death pounces on him even as he still procrastinates and harbors false hopes.

Success is from God; He is the Helper.

THIRD CIRCLE

This is the path of *Iḥsān*, the transition from outward to inward, from knowledge and evidence to tasting and experience. When *Islām* and *Īmān* are mastered by the servant and he acquires an adequate portion of those legal sciences mentioned in the Book and *Sunna*, his knowledge broadens, his understanding is unshackled, and his breast expands. He comes to know himself and thus to know his Lord and seek His satisfaction and nearness. He sees his own weakness, abasement, extreme neediness, and ignorance, for he was created, as were all the worlds, from nothingness and is returning to nothingness, utterly needy and necessitous, possessing no independent power, no power of choice, no existence, no subsistence, no favors, no gifts, save from Him whose existence is necessary and on whom he depends for all things. His very existence and its sustaining, every perfection he has, every action and reaction, even his sitting down and standing up, are favors and gifts from God. He will thus recognize the bounties that God has bestowed upon him and that it is by His favor, Transcendent is He, that he is given to thank and remember Him in each act of obedience and excellence. Hence he will not demand to be rewarded for them, nor will he look at them; he will be frightened by their presence and his defectiveness in giving thanks for them. These thanks are none other than to witness and acknowledge them as favors. When he comes to know his Lord thus, he will fear Him, hope in Him, constantly utter His remembrance, observe His prohibitions, obey His orders, and seek His proximity. He will experience an overwhelming wish to return to Him and an increasing love for Him. He will then establish himself firmly in that and continue to taste and experience until he comes to worship God as if he were seeing Him[01] and will perceive the meaning that He intends and shows him. He will acknowledge that God has favored him with His obedience and remembrance, and confess his inability to fulfill His rights and thank Him. He will then flee from all the worlds to God and renounce the attribution of importance to both obedience and disobedience, and he will taste *Lā ḥawla wa lā quwwata illā bi-Llāh*, 'there is neither strength nor ability save by God'. He will continue to rise in the waystations of patience, gratitude, and humility, and will drink from the fountain of contentment, surrender, reliance and love. He will then surrender all his affairs to God and hand over to Him control over whatever has been granted him of the things of both this world and the Next, so that He may take over. He will travel in God, fleeing to Him, freed from all restraint in His remembrance, engrossed in Him, until he becomes extinct to himself and his *dhikr* and drowned in Him. He will lose his perception of others and may be so utterly lost in Him that he may speak with the tongue of the Real and might then say, 'I am the Real!' He may also deny his separate existence among creation. He is to be excused, for he is under the powerful sway of *Ḥaqīqa* and is oscillating between sobriety and inebriation, union and separation, presence to himself and absence, until he realizes existence and is given the investiture of generosity. Then his proximity becomes sound and his love clear, and God becomes his hearing with which he hears, his sight with which he sees, his hand with which he grasps, and his foot on which he walks; when he seeks His protection He will protect him and when he asks of Him He will give him[52]. At that point the Lights of Reality will shine upon him, and he will taste the reaping of the meanings of Revelation and Prophethood in the stations of nearness, election, and chivalry (*futuwwa*). He will contemplate

01 A reference to the *ḥadīth* in which the Prophet ﷺ defines excellence or *Iḥsān* as: *to worship God as though you see Him, for if you do not see Him, He sees you.* [Bukhārī, *Ṣaḥīḥ*, 50].

the realities of Revelation in detail and know the sciences of principles and applications. He will understand by God from God every problem and will see clearly, by His light, through every enigma.

That is the fruition of *taqwā*, certitude, and company of the men of God, the pious. God the Exalted says, **And he who fears God, He will appoint for him a way out**, from everything problematic or enigmatic, **and He will provide for him**, knowledge and understanding, **from whence he expects not.**[53] And He also says, **Fear God and God will teach you.**[54] **If you fear God, He will grant you discernment.**[55]

Success is from God.

FOURTH CIRCLE

This is beholding the higher realities (*ḥaqā'iq*) and identifying the limits and places of ascent for all subtle (*raqā'iq*) and fine realities (*daqā'iq*).[01] This is the fruition of the Path, the cream of realization. He who is to be granted success, when he holds on firmly to his Qur'ānic *wāridāt* and to the Muḥammadan Sunna, according to the dictates of excellence (*Iḥsān*), and is assisted by solicitude from his Lord, becomes firmly established in contemplation and witnesses the diffusion of the reality of liberality in all the channels of existence and creation[02]. He will see and hear the truth as truth; he will know right from wrong, and follow it. His path will be illumined by the light of truth and his outward form will be upright according to the scales of justice. His reality will become clear with the limpidity of certitude; then complete illumination will dawn upon him and perfect humanity will manifest through him. His secret will be with God the Exalted in the holiness of the *Lāhūt*, his heart with the Supreme Assembly in the highest *Malakūt*, and his body worshiping God with other men of God in the world of the *Nāsūt*[03].

---

01 *Ḥaqā'iq*, translated here as higher realities, probably indicates the subtle images of the *Malakūt*, so that *raqā'iq* will mean the realities of the *jabarūt* or formless spiritual world, and *daqā'iq* the realities of the Names and Attributes.

02 The reality of Divine liberality is to give before being asked. Its main manifestation is the bestowal of existence on created beings. This gift, which is renewed every single instant, suffuses the entire creation.

03 *Nāsūt*, from *nās*: the visible world of mankind. *Malakūt*: The world of subtle forms,

He will worship God with the acts of worship of all created beings. In his remembrance he will be with the *Karrūbiyyūn*[01], in his *tasbīḥ* and reflection with the Near Angels[02], and his good works and gratitude with the righteous servants of God. He will thus have remembered God with the praises of all creatures, stood in humility with the universals, and bowed and prostrated himself in his various stages with those who are in prostration. Through guidance his soul finds comfort in certitude. His natural appetites and his angry predatory drives have submitted to him and to religion, his devil has become a Muslim and is now a helper in righteousness. He is looked upon with the Divine eye of solicitude and protected by His looking after him to the full. Whenever the favors of God upon him increase, so that he is granted to obey and remember Him, and know His majesty, greatness, lofty power and invincibility, he becomes even more aware of his own shortcomings and neglectfulness in thanking Him, and he confesses his powerlessness, poverty and evanescence. He thus asks forgiveness more than a hundred times a day and fears God more than do sinners, because he now knows Him ﷻ, and how He is. His fear and submission to the majesty of the Compeller is greater than his fear of retaliation and torment in the Fire, for the Fire is but one of His creatures, one of His slaves carrying out His will in His creation, and He knows what He has that is even more awesome: **and none knows the hosts of your Lord but He**[56]**; and He creates that which you know not**[57]**; He is not to be questioned as to what He does**[58]**; To God belongs the ultimate argument**[59]**; and to God belongs the supreme example**[60]**; and above each one endowed with knowledge is one more knowledgeable**[61].

This servant, by now destined to succeed, remains between the fear of trials and afflictions and the hope for nearness and benefaction, both here and now, and later on in the Garden. At one time he is constricted by Majesty, at another soothed by Beauty. Every single attribute of his testifies to his poverty and he beholds blessings and gifts in every circumstance.

intermediary between the dense physical and the formless luminous worlds. *Lāhūt*: The Names, Attributes and Essence of God.

01 These are the Highest Angels, *al-ʿĀlūn*, those who are devoted to the glorification of their Lord to the exclusion of all else and are unaware of the existence of the created universe.

02 These are the angels of the Supreme Council, *al-Mala' al-Aʿlā*, among whom are Seraphiel, Gabriel, Michael, and Azrael.

His sciences are those of the Qur'ān and Sunna. He delves into their arts, fathoms their depths, delights in their lights, rejoices in their secrets, drinks the beverage of their fountains, and dives for their jewels and secrets. The contemplation of reality veils him neither from the rulings of *Sharīʿa*, nor from the vision of creation. Good works are for him gifts from God and bounties; granted by Him that he may approach Him by means of them, unlocked by Him that He may increase him. They are the door to God and none can enter to Him save through it; there is no other passage. He works according to his nearness and the graces he is shown, upholds the obligations of *Sharīʿa*, believing that even when no longer tiresome they are still incumbent. He fears falling into sin and remoteness even when his nearness, intimacy, and amicability are well established. He is the comprehensive slave of God, the manifestation of His shining secret, the one who summons to Him clear-sightedly, the provider for creation by Him for Him of everything outward or inward. Should God reveal him [to creation], it is by His grace that he will appear. Through him His favors and mercy reach those He wishes, according to what He has apportioned by way of good fortune and what He has decreed by way of impregnation and childbirth[01]. **He gives to whom He will females, and He gives to whom He will males, or He couples them, both males and females, and He makes whom He will barren; truly He is the All-Knowing, the All-Powerful**[02].

CONCLUSION

There is no opposition between outward and inward, first and last, or *Sharīʿa*, *Ṭarīqa* and *Ḥaqīqa*. The explanation of this is that *Sharīʿa* is the prescription that God has charged [His] servants with, so that they obey Him and submit, even while secondary causes are affirmed and acts are attributed to created beings, that He may extricate them from the darkness of passion

---

01 Here spiritual transmission is likened to physical impregnation. The further spiritual development of the traveler leads to the opening which is the birth of the child of direct knowledge, the potential for which he had been carrying within himself.

02 Qur'ān, 42:49,50, **He gives to whom He will females**, who represent the outward knowledge of *Sharīʿa*, **and He gives to whom He will males**, who represent the inward knowledge of *ḥaqīqa*, **or He couples them, both males and females**, making them perfect masters, equally well versed in both outward and inward knowledge.

and nature by the rule of *Sharīʿa*, by avoiding what is prohibited and doing what is prescribed in every matter.

Ṭarīqa is to travel by this *Sharīʿa* to God, as proficiently as is practicable, maintaining sincerity towards Him, with total concentration, and renouncing one's dependence on secondary causes. Attributing [everything to God] leads to abandoning the shackles and constraints [of secondary causes] for the place where Divine generosity appears, the source of all existence.

Ḥaqīqa is the manifestation of the Real by His light to His servant, by the realization of utmost transcendence, together with the appearance of Unicity (*waḥdāniyya*), free of either neutralization (*taʿṭīl*), or anthropomorphism (*tashbīh*)[01].

Let us clarify this by using example of the 'attribution of actions'. God, by His unique determinative power, creates the servant, his ability, and his acts. Therefore the attribution of actions to God is *Ḥaqīqa*. To attribute them to the servant because God has done so is *Sharīʿa*. For the servant to use his own ability to act while seeing the act originating in his Lord without contradiction is *Ṭarīqa*. When God the Exalted says, You threw not, this is *Ṭarīqa*. When He says, when you threw', this is *Sharīʿa*; when He says, but God threw[62], this is *Ḥaqīqa*.

When the servant says, for example, 'I will pray', this is *Sharīʿa*. When he says, 'I will pray by God', this is *Ṭarīqa*. And when he says, 'God prays on behalf of me', meaning 'He creates the prayer in me and attributes it to me', this is *Ḥaqīqa*.

Another example is the human being. He has a visible body, an animal spirit and an invisible soul[02]. His speaking soul is to all appearances opposed to his body, for it is subtle and radiant, transcending form and description. The animal spirit is the bridge between them for it shares with each some

---

01 Neutralization (*taʿṭīl*) is figurative interpretation of Divine Attributes, with the intention of preserving His transcendence, taken so far as to render them inoperative. Its opposite, anthropomorphism (*tashbīh*), is the ascription of formal, human-like attributes to God, by literally interpreting texts which are manifestly figurative. The creed of *Ahl al Sunna wa al-Jamāʿa* stands between these two extremes.

02 The animal spirit is the vital energy that is closest to the material body and keeps it alive. The speaking soul is that subtle part of the human being which reasons and feels emotions. It is dependent upon the spirit of pure light, which is highest in the hierarchy composing the human being but is sometimes identified with the 'speaking soul'.

of their attributes. The whole is one human being. Similarly, *Sharīʿa* and *Ḥaqīqa*, together with *Ṭarīqa* are one religion, one all-embracing unit. It is like attributing the same act both to God and the servant, for all power belongs to God and to Him do all matters return. He is the First and the Last, the Outward and the Inward, and He has the knowledge of everything[63]. He is a Witness to everything, He embraces all things, and He is Able to do all things. To God do all things surely return,[64] whether they be of this world or the next, whether they be the bestowal of gifts or of existence itself, whether they be witnesses or witnessed.

Transcendent is He who has caused everything to appear by His light, for He is the light of the heavens and the earth. Were it not for His light surrounding everything, nothing would have appeared. He is more apparent than everything else, so let no one imagine that He is hidden or veiled—for to be veiled is to be overcome, and He is the All-Prevailing. Rather, it is created beings that are veiled from seeing themselves and the darkness of the worlds that surround them.

This is how the Divine matter is as concerns the ability to act and also other attributes and states such as hearing, vision, and speech; subsistence and extinction; union and separation; firmness and dispersion; and time and place, as concerns both the essence of each of these and its attributes.

Those who deny and those who are ignorant may misunderstand these things and attribute the beliefs of incarnation, union, and deviation to people who are blameless and are guilty neither of error nor of swerving away from the truth. Far be it from the people of religion, knowledge, certitude and perfection! He will know this and acknowledge it who is fair-minded and accepts the statements of authorities in matters of creed and what they have stated concerning the question of speech: that the Qur'ān is the Speech of God, preserved in hearts, heard by ears, written in the *muṣḥaf* but not contained by it. Similarly, the appearance of the act of [God's] servant, wrought by his contingent power, is of no consequence when the reality of the act is attributed to God. For the [human] faculty is but the locus of manifestation of the divine omnipotence in creating actions, just as the *muṣḥaf*, letters, ears and hearts are but locuses of the manifestations of the Speech of God in them.

This knowledge is a slippery slope for the reckless. For him who has not mastered the legal sciences, those of the path, and the ways of reality, with knowledge, taste and mastery, it is more appropriate to avoid this and refrain from delving into it. Only he is able to grasp it whose heart God has illumined, whose mind He has disciplined, whose breast He has expanded with certitude, so that his condition in relation to God has become sound. We should not have mentioned it in this context, were it not for the wish to arouse yearning for it, to praise and laud it for being the treasury of riches and the worthiest of all things to be striven for and attended to. But it is also the most deserving of being kept hidden and thoroughly protected, to be dispensed only to the élite, the people of tasting and sincerity. Otherwise, it is much better to expound outward knowledge, especially that of the Book, Sunna, and what follows, and to base upon these *Fiqh*, and Sufism, which embellish it and make it pleasurable to the ear[01]. This is far less likely to lead to innovation in following the Messenger, more likely to provide firm foundations for principles and soundness for applications. The knowledge of the Book and *Sunna* will thus become what the person knows and does, understanding religion his prime interest and main mental activity, Sufism his path and hallmark, and reality his treasure and the secret which he will be keeping.

Let this be the termination and conclusion of this model. God knows best. May God's blessings and peace be upon our Master Muḥammad, his family and his Companions. All Praise belongs to God.

---

01 *Fiqh* is said by the Sufis to be dry, so they sometimes expand it a little during teaching to include some spirituality, which embellishes it and makes it more acceptable to students' ears.

Unveiling The Truth

UNVEILING THE TRUTH OF THE SCIENCES OF REALITY

AND REMOVING CONFUSION FROM THE PRACTICES OF THE PATH

(*KASHF AL-ḤAQQ ʿAN ʿULŪM AL-ḤAQĪQA WA TAMYĪZ*

AL-TALBĪS ʿAN RUSŪM AL-ṬARĪQA)

Preface

The following short treatise by Ḥabīb ʿAbd al-Raḥmān Balfaqīh consists of his answers to four questions from four different people, three of whom wrote to him in 1135/1722. They are all concerned with aspects of Sufism which have preoccupied travelers on the Path for centuries. For the Path inevitably brings one up against obscure and ambiguous situations and then their clarification by a true master becomes a necessity.

In the Name of God, Most Merciful and Compassionate

All praises and thanks are for God, the All-Near who responds[01] to those who have questions; the Opener who well knows how every bestowal will be received by its recipient, according to the dictates of the latter's realities and his capacity to receive[02]; the Bestower who always accords every desired thing to all who respond and all who ask[03]; who gathers and then

01 This refers to the two Divine Names *al-Qarīb al-Mujīb*, the Near and the Responsive, which are usually used together in *duʿā'*; for he who prays needs to remind himself that he is calling upon Him who is so near that He can clearly hear his complaint and request, see his condition, read his mind, feel his feelings, and is sure to respond in the best possible manner.

02 The recipient, *al-qābil*, receives everything that comes to him from the higher worlds according to his aptitude, which consists in his qualities, limits, and needs. Spiritual things are according to spiritual aptitude, and intellectual, physical, social, and other things according to their respective aptitudes.

03 God is more likely to accord desired things to those who, before asking Him for what they desire, have responded to His call, believed in Him as He wishes them to and obeyed His injunctions.

divides among His servants what He will, in any manner He will, of His abundant assistance and favors. I praise Him with the profoundest praises ever uttered by the most veracious speaker.

I beseech Him by His all-embracing liberality, which is the best of pretexts[01], and by His perfect chosen servant, our Master Muḥammad, his noble Family, magnificent Companions, and exemplary Followers.

To proceed: I have received in this year of 1135 three questions which, although from areas far apart, have arrived at almost the same time, and bear some resemblance to each other in meaning as concerns their principles[02], details, and proofs. This is why the answer to them was given all at once.

The circumstances, the dictates of the truth, and the need to correct the statements of every speaker require the establishment of principles from which will branch out in chapters the answers and that which relates to them, so that the truth may become clear to whoever cares to speak of these and similar matters to the one who has posed the question and to everyone else. Thus, by the truth will the clear way be made obvious, and also how much confusion have the people of false claims caused concerning the practices of the Path and the sciences of realities[03], applied to every quality and attribute.

I have entitled it *Unveiling the Truth of the Sciences of Reality and Removing the Confusion from the Practices of the Path.* It is one of the best treatises on the subject, includes everything that is needed, and is divided into a prologue, a conclusion, and ten chapters that provide a detailed exposition of its purposes and its proofs.

---

01 "Pretext" is used here for *wasīla*, that which is so important that God can be besought by it: in this case His own Attribute of liberality, then His Beloved Messenger, Muhammad ﷺ.

02 Principles, *Uṣūl*, are all-inclusive laws. Principles pertain to synthetic as opposed to analytic knowledge. Synthetic knowledge is to know in sum, not in detail. The more comprehensive the principle, the higher ranking it becomes. Analytic knowledge, termed *furūʿ* (branches) in Arabic, is the knowledge of details and their applications. Any science must have both principles and details or applications, or in other words roots and branches.

03 The practices of the Path constitute the Science of the Path, the *Ṭarīqa*, the Method. As for the Science of Realities, it is the science of what one sees after the struggle against the ego has led to the Opening.

PROLOGUE

Here we shall quote the questions in the very words of the questioner, and the reasons and motives for answering.

The first question is from a brother from the auspicious Yemen who says:

'What do you say, *sayyidī wa qurrat ʿaynī*[01], of someone these days who has set himself to train spiritual disciples and guide on the Path those who come to him, according to the dictates of the People of the Path[02], which are the essence of religion and the prerogative of the people of certainty, when this is a precious Path the traces of which are fading, and a noble dwelling the fire of which is dying out and the secrets of which have become even more hidden?

We find in the writings of many authoritative scholars and great Knowers, who have joined their knowledge of illumination and their tasting of the secrets[03] to mastery of the outward sciences, such as the Proof of Islam al-Ghazālī and others from the early generations, and Shaykh ʿAbd al-Wahhāb al-Shaʿrānī and those like him from the latecomers, impressive expositions of the sources[04] of the components of this Path and of all its details. Now according to the prevailing conditions, we must conclude

01 *Sayyidī* means 'my master'. It is a term of respect used by a son to address his father and uncles, a student to address his teacher, and everyone to address the descendants of the Prophet ﷺ. In the vernacular it becomes *sīdī*, which is in common usage. *Qurrat ʿaynī* literally means 'the repose of my eyes', or as some prefer, 'the coolness of my eyes'. It is used to denote someone or something which brings serene satisfaction.

02 By 'dictates of the People of the Path' is meant the Science of the Path or of the Method.

03 The term 'tasting' or *dhawq* is used by the Sufis to indicate the direct experience of the Unseen, which for those possessed of unveiling and contemplation is as immediate as tasting is in the physical realm.

04 The sources meant here are the textual origins of the practices of the Sufi path in the Qur'ān and Sunna, and the legal principles drawn from them.

that they are impossible to realize, so that rationally speaking, we are almost certain that the way to this Path[01] is today blocked and any claims of realization are today to be rejected. Also, we observe that most of those shouldering such tasks nowadays are lacking in knowledge and mediocre in works; they have not tasted and have too little light to solve the problems facing them. Furthermore, they are evidently greedy for what other people possess and have made the adoption of the formal practices of this Path a net with which to catch the social eminence and accumulation of debris they desire, and are thus deceiving the common people. Most of them have succeeded their fathers, friends, or brothers, and then they exceed their limits and wrong others, driven by their pride in their growing entourage, numerous followers, and the speed with which the common people gather around them.

Therefore, remove for us the veil over this disquieting matter, *sayyidī*! Open for us the door to the way to this Path, and how to escape this distress and save oneself from this dark tenebrous situation.

He who is posing the question and loves you has carried his inquiry about this quandary all over Syria and the Yemen, but has found none in these times more worthy than you to provide a solution and an answer, for you have combined in your outward religious knowledge the rational and the revealed[02], and have qualified in the Path to expound both the principles and the branches. What has already appeared of your authority is more than sufficient and convincing, and it expounds the Truth and the Path both outwardly and inwardly.

I ask God to look after you outwardly and inwardly, guard you with the eye of His solicitude and His most special protection, and protect through you both the élite and the common people from all the lures that lead astray and all injurious misfortunes.'[03]

---

01 The questioner is speaking not of the Sufi Path itself, but of the path to it. The Sufi Path begins once one has found a true master, pledged one's allegiance to him, and started the Path's practices under his guidance. The path to the Path, then, is presumably the quest for such a master, the search for a true Knower who has attained the Great Opening and is capable of guiding others along the same route.

02 The rational, *al-ʿAqlī*, is that which is acquired by philosophical reasoning and logical deduction, while that which is revealed, or handed-down or transmitted, *al-Naqlī*, is the knowledge of the Qur'ān and *Sunna* received by sound transmission.

03 This first question is thus about spiritual masters and how to differentiate between

The second question is from a gentleman from India and concerns a certain man who discourses with the tongue of the people of realities and that of the direct experiences of the people of the Path, before whom are read the books of realities, and who spreads them abroad publicly among crowds including the insincere, as well as the sincere, the derogatory adversary, and the acquiescent believer. He claims that this is the real religion, the mark of the people of certainty, and the cream of the qualities of the God-fearing. We see one of our teachers, whose spiritual state is greater, whose efforts are more arduous, and whose works are more upright, forbidding this, keeping away from it, and warning against engaging in it. He believes it to be more important to concern oneself with the science of transactions[01], exert oneself in improving one's performance in acts of worship, and persevere in praying in congregation. He also thinks that to speak of matters exclusive to the élite to the common people is disastrous, an error that can cause widespread damage.

'Please answer this question, *sayyidī*, and remove the obscurity from this problem, for people have split in two groups on this issue, and we now depend on you and address in earnest our request to you; so succor us with what we desire and explain where the truth lies with clear evidence and clear instructions.

May God preserve you for the benefit of the people, as a light to enlighten the seekers of the truth everywhere, and may He make you a landmark for the people of religion and a leader for the God-fearing on the path of right guidance.'

This question was also asked by the first questioner in rather similar terms, but he also quoted some of the utterances of the person whose state and discourse he asked about[02].

The third question is from a scholar from Makka the Honorable.

'What do you say, *sayyidī wa ḥabībī fī Allāh*, upon whom, after God and His Messenger, I rely as concerns God's religion, of those who are counted

---

real, underqualified, and fake ones, a very real practical problem facing those who wish to start on the Path.

01 The Science of Transactions, *ʿIlm al-Muʿāmala*, is knowledge of the Sacred Law, as distinct from the Science of Unveiling, *ʿIlm al-Mukāshafa*, which is the knowledge of inward states and secrets.

02 The second question is about the wisdom and legality of discoursing on the Sufi science of realities in public.

among the people of the Path of these days and at whose hands some supernatural events occur, and who possess certain powers to affect things, for instance some followers of our master the famous Shaykh Aḥmad ibn ʿIlwān, and those attached to our master the great Shaykh Aḥmad al-Rifāʿī, the choice of the Most Merciful? For the common people are won over by their stabbing themselves without any deleterious effect, handling snakes, walking on fires, and other such things as are done by the *fuqarā'* of these times. However, anyone who looks into their conditions and observes their behavior finds them opposed to the well-known things of religion, diverging from the path of the God-fearing, and opposed to the rules of Sufism and certainty. On the contrary, they are more likely to resemble the conditions of impostors and the states of the corrupt and the sinful.

Therefore, please explain to us in unambiguous terms what this is which they exhibit around, and guide us to how we should array our evidence, arguments, and proofs. Remove this harm from the path of the élite who are attached to the people of direct knowledge[01]. We have searched long for this and inquired among many venerable well-known persons and those known to be the guides to the truth of these times; and they have directed us to address our request to God, then to you. Since they referred us to you alone for an answer to this problem, you are left with no option but to provide us with the answer, for this duty has now fallen exclusively to you.

May God preserve you as an all-embracing benefit for the people of this time, an exemplar, and a recourse in every difficulty for the people of this business[02].'

These three questions I have quoted verbatim so that those who read the answer, both those who agree and those who do not, will know the harm done that the questioner so clearly describes, for harm is indeed being done, and deception by it is widespread, but none is answering or refuting it. It is therefore my duty to reveal what I have concerning this, the knowledge

---

01 Muslim, *Ṣaḥīḥ*, 58. *Faith has over seventy branches; the best is saying* Lā ilāha illā Allāh, *and the lowest is to remove harm from the road; and modesty is a branch of faith.*

02 This question is about the followers of certain Sufi *Ṭarīqa*s who indulge in seemingly supernatural acts such as stabbing themselves, handling venomous snakes, and walking on live coals. These things induce the general public to believe that they are great saints, whereas they are seen not to be knowledgeable in religious matters, nor to properly observe the rulings of the Sacred Law. In fact, although some of them may be real Sufis, the great majority are far from anything resembling Sufism.

that I have, and the understanding I was given. I have hesitated long before answering, thinking that silence was safer and more profitable than opening things up, because incapacity, mediocrity, and deviation now predominate, and there is an abundance of people who deny and are jealous and hostile to such things, and who obstinately oppose those who open this door[01]. But I saw that the truth is evident by itself and not from the men, and those who are fair consider what is being said, not who is saying it.[02]

Should God grant us success in stating the truth, it is by His grace, and if I fall into error, I confess that I am inadequate and inherently so.

The degree of perfection belongs only to him who was selected by God and granted the reality of infallibility in all his attributes[03].

A fourth question: I have added to these three questions a fourth which was sent to me a long time ago and I have already answered, but is in the same vein as the others and its answer resembles theirs in both principles and details. It is also from Yemen.

The questioner says, 'What do you say, *sayyidī*, about the things that are attributed to people of God, people of tasting and true unveiling and certainty[04], such as the question of the 'unity of existence' and of manifestation in forms, as reported of Shaykh Muḥyī al-Dīn [Ibn al-ʿArabī], his famous saying concerning the question of 'acquisition', and the ambiguous verses where meanings are derived without limitations or determination? Does this contradict what the majority of authoritative scholars and meticulous experts on beliefs agree upon? Or is there no contradiction in reality, but

---

01 Two kinds of problems may arise from an open discussion of such matters. The first is that the general public is far from qualified to understand both logical and textual arguments. The general level of religious education is very low, yet teachers find people indifferent and even resistant to learning, and prone to follow their emotions and passions and so go off course. The second problem is active opposition from *Salafī*s and *Wahhābī*s whose superficial argumentation and misuse of textual evidence easily deceives those who are not well versed in knowledge.

02 This is a famous saying of Imām ʿAlī, may God be pleased with him: 'Know the men by the truth, not the truth by the men. Know the truth and you will know its people.' To this scholars later added, 'Look what is being said, not who is saying it.'

03 The degree of perfection belongs to the Prophet ﷺ. He was chosen for it by God and given total infallibility in all attributes.

04 By these are meant the Knowers by God who speak of nothing unless they have direct experience of it.

only in appearance, according to the knowledge, deductions, unveiling, and tasting of the people of the Path?'[01]

The answer

We shall start, with God's permission, to answer according to the knowledge that God causes to overflow over intellects, the openings He grants to understand handed-down knowledge, and the confirmation of these from the words of the authoritative sages of the Path and the experts on principles.[02] We ask of God that we may attain what we ask for and gain what we desire. As for the principles:

First Principle

It is well-known that discoursing on any particular subject is a branch of having conceived of it in sum, and grasped its essence, again in sum and not in detail, for the unknown cannot be sought[03]. Any particular subject can neither be confirmed, denied, accepted, or rejected, unless it becomes known. Before its branches one must know its principles, since one cannot recognize the branches unless one establishes the principles and identifies the rules one should fall back on and the consequences in terms of necessary preconditions and consequent behavior.

Now if anyone who discourses on any specialty within any science does not connect its branches to its principles as known to him, ascertain in turn its principle from its relation to its branches, join to his rational effort authentic transmission, and then compare his conclusions to what he finds

---

01 This last question is about the sciences of reality spoken of earlier, and here the questioner mentions explicitly the thorny problems of *waḥdat al-wujūd* or unity of existence, and of *kasb* (the doctrine that human acts are 'acquired'), and the Sufi interpretations of the ambiguous verses of the Qur'ān. Are these legitimate expositions of the concepts contained in the religious sciences, albeit in more depth than most people are able to understand, or do they contradict them?

02 The author is requesting assistance from God in both the knowledge that depends on transmission and that which depends on the rational operation of the mind. He seeks the illumination of his intelligence by inspiration both to understand textual evidence as it should be understood, and that when he exerts his intelligence, it is in a sound manner, so as to allow him to reach conclusions that conform to the truth.

03 By 'the unknown' is meant here the endless details of the subject, for the human mind was created capable of grasping wholes, summations, and generalities, but incapable of grasping all the details of any particular subject.

explicitly on record by the experts, then it is better for him to keep silent and avoid trying to solve its problems or unravel its difficulties, for once he starts identifying its divisions and investigating its principles, branches, and divisions, error will be much nearer to him than truth, unless he confines himself to mere rehearsal of what has already been said and what he has received from the masters of transmission; for it may happen that someone will carry knowledge who is not himself knowledgeable, or that one who receives [the knowledge] understands less than one who hears it from him[01].

There is no doubt that the science of Sufism, which includes the sciences of 'subtle things that soften the heart' (*Raqā'iq*) and of spiritual realities (*Ḥaqā'iq*)[02], is the essence of religion, the cream of its sciences. Its derivation from the sciences of religion, and their acquisition being a precondition for its soundness, are well-known, for it is their essence and perfect fruit[03]. To discourse on its with authority and in detail requires knowledge of the principle and branches, and the acquisition of an abundant amount of both rational and transmitted sciences, together with an acute intelligence, an aptitude consisting in a sound heart and a pure soul, in someone whose belief is untainted, possessed of taste and a fullness of light, free from fanaticism and other impediments and personal intentions, and free from all arbitrariness or vengeful and critical drives.

Sufism is in reality an understanding of religion, the acquisition of the attributes of the God-fearing, and striving to strengthen certainty. It is thus built on the Science of Legal Rules and their principles and branches,

---

01 This is a *ḥadīth* which is in Tirmidhī, *Sunan*, 2656, and other compilations. *It may happen that one will carry knowledge who is not himself knowledgeable.* The other *ḥadīth*, which states *It may happen that one who receives [knowledge] understands less than one who hears it from him*, is in Bukhārī, *Ṣaḥīḥ*, 1741, and other compilations.

02 *Ḥaqā'iq* is the plural of *Ḥaqīqa*, which means reality, while *Raqā'iq* is the plural of *Raqīqa*, which means subtleties. The science of realities, whose most famous exponent is Shaykh Muḥyī al-Dīn Ibn al-ʿArabī, is the science of what is witnessed after the struggle against the ego has led to the Opening; whereas the science of *Ṭarīqa*, which is the science of the Method, or as Imām Ghazālī calls it, the science of Transactions, *ʿIlm al-Muʿāmala*, is everything that comes before that and leads up to it.

03 Sufism, being the road to the ultimate aim of religion which is the direct knowledge of God, is the result of practicing the religious sciences to the full. The acquisition and practice of the latter are therefore preconditions for the practice of Sufism to be sound.

on *ḥadīth*, and Qur'ānic exegesis, which are in turn built on the other sciences[01], as every experienced expert is aware, together with an addition upon which depends the science of Sufism, which is the science of good character and the secret aspects of people, upon which are built most of the rules of the path.[02] Even higher is the clear appearance of the truth and of the various manifestations of creation, by the contemplation of the lights and the tasting of the secrets of reality, which is the goal [of Sufism] for those who know it in depth.[03]

Second Principle

Sufism is a special kind of *Fiqh* or Sacred Law, for the Science of Legal Rules called *Fiqh* and its various branches are general rules, according to the dictates of Islam, for everyone in general, including both the élite and the common people[04]. Its rulings are general and inclusive, whereas the rules of Sufism are special for special cases and are exclusive to the élite[05]. This

---

01 By Science of Legal Rules is meant Jurisprudence or *Fiqh*, which is based on Qur'ān and *ḥadīth*, which in turn needs, in order to be properly understood, the ancillary sciences which are termed *al-ālāt*, the 'tools': primarily Arabic and its various sciences such as grammar, semantics, and rhetoric, and secondarily history, genealogy, logic, etc.

02 Expert knowledge of the human soul, its good and evil qualities, its passions and appetites, and its secrets, is necessary in Sufism, since it is upon this that the rules of wayfaring are based.

03 The gist of this principle is that to discourse on any particular subject, such as the science of Sufism with its two divisions of *Raqā'iq* and *Ḥaqā'iq*, one must know its principles. Expertise in Sufism requires not only knowledge but also aptitude of the heart. Knowledge of its principle and branches must be mastered from its sources, which are Revelation with all its sciences and the logical operations of the rational mind. The requirements for this mastery are an adequate intelligence and a soul pure in its beliefs, character, and behavior. The third source of knowledge, which is spiritual openings, comes about as a result of achieving mastery in the first two and purifying the heart.

04 This means that the rules of *Sharī'a* as detailed in the Science of *Fiqh* apply to the first level of the ternary *Islām*, *Īmān*, *Iḥsān*, namely Islam, for they include the outward legal observances and are to be applied to every Muslim indiscriminately.

05 Sufism is the application of the Sacred Law in a special manner, with maximum effort and sincerity, observing the inward, which is the heart, as well as the outward, and is therefore practiced exclusively by those who have devoted themselves entirely to the quest for God, and those are the Sufis.

means that the same ruling will differ in its application to different people according to their condition and circumstances[01], and what the time and relationships necessitate. Thus no general or permanent ruling can be issued, but only according to the condition of every particular person and that of his particular time and place. This is why here the mere teacher (*Shaykh al-Taʿlīm*) is not sufficient, for he only gives general discourses. It is the master of discipline (*Shaykh al-Tarbiya*) who is required, for his observations are more precise, he can ascertain and distinguish between things, and he can decide on priorities according to changing circumstances.

Once you realize this, you will realize that the special is included in the general, so that every Sufism is *Fiqh*, for *Fiqh* is but rules, but not every *Fiqh* is Sufism.[02]

Ṭarīqa, the Method, is to practice *Sharīʿa,* the Sacred Law, in a special manner and under special conditions. *Ḥaqīqa*, Reality, is the fruit of *Ṭarīqa*, and can but conform to *Sharīʿa,* since it depends and is based on it. It is therefore inevitable that *Ḥaqīqa* should conform to the Qur'ān and Sunna. Thus every *Ḥaqīqa* not based on *Ṭarīqa* and confirmed by *Sharīʿa* is to be rejected; and every path not coming from the Qur'ān and *Sunna* is blocked. **Religion with God is Islam**[65]**; He who seeks other than Islam for a religion, it will not be accepted from him**[66]**; Say, 'This is my path; I summon to God, clear-sightedly, I and those who follow me**[67]. And we find in *ḥadīth*s: *He who adds to this concern of ours anything that does not belong to it is to be rejected*[68]. *So keep to my* Sunna *and that of the rightly-guided wise successors after me, bite on it tightly with your teeth*[69]. *Beware of innovations, for every innovation is an error and every error is in the Fire*[70]. There are other similar verses and *Ḥadīth*s.

The Formidable Qur'ān is a criterion that distinguishes between truth and falsehood; a guiding light to recognizing the learned from the ignorant; a fair balance to distinguish between the superior and the more superior,

01 By 'condition' is meant the state of the heart and the attributes of the soul, whereas by 'circumstances' are meant the conditions of the outer environment, including events affecting the person.

02 This means that Sufism, being the application of *Sharīʿa* in a special way, which is total sincerity and depth, is for special people—that is, as mentioned above, for those who have devoted entirely to the quest for God. This special manner of applying the *Sharīʿa* so as to extract maximum proficiency from it is obviously exclusive to the élite.

what is rising and what is falling. It is, together with the Noble *Sunna*, which is its explanation and clarification, a judge over what anyone may say or do, and to it are all questions of rulings and problems to be referred at times of disagreement. He ﷻ says, **And if you disagree on something, refer it to God and His Messenger**[71]. And He says, **This Qur'ān guides to the way most upright**[72]. He ﷻ says also, **And he who follows My guidance shall suffer neither error nor wretchedness.**[73] And He ﷻ says, **Say, 'God's guidance is the guidance'**[74]. He ﷻ says also, **Follow what has been sent down to you from your Lord and do not follow other allies than Him.**[75] There many other similar verses. And He ﷻ says, **And We have sent down the Remembrance upon you that you may make clear to people what is sent down to them.**[76] He ﷻ says also, **And he speaks not out of caprice; it is but revelation revealed.**[77]And He ﷻ says, **And what the Messenger brings you accept and what he forbids you forsake.**[78]

And he ﷺ said, *I have left with you that which if you hold on fast to you will never err: The Book of God and my* Sunna[79]. *Let the Qur'ān speak through my* Sunna, *for your eyes will never go blind, nor will your feet slip, nor will your hand be too short, so long as you follow them*[80]. He also said, *The best discourse is the Book of God and the best guidance the guidance of Muḥammad. The worst things are innovations and every innovation is an error.*[81] He also said, *Why do some people avoid certain things that I do? By God, I am the one who knows God best and fears Him most!*[82] He also said, *I have been given the Qur'ān and as much with it. Soon, a satiated man, reclining on his couch, will say, 'This Qur'ān should suffice you; what you find licit in it, treat as licit, and what you find illicit, treat as illicit.' But what the Messenger of God forbids is just like what God forbids. . .*[83] And other such verses and *Ḥadīth*s, which impose on all Muslims not to accept or submit to, save that which is confirmed by the Book and Sunna—and to disregard any [mere] opinion, whether it be held by a man of knowledge and deduction or by a man of Sufism manifestly possessed of tasting and unveiling. For it is agreed by all that logical deduction may fail as well as succeed, and unveiling, if outside the limits of the Book and Sunna, is unsound and must not be accepted; for true unveiling does not exceed the limits of the Book and *Sunna*, being the result of conformity to religion and following [the Prophet]. *Sharīʿa* is the outward of *Ḥaqīqa*, and *Ḥaqīqa* the inward of *Sharīʿa*. They are inseparable, so that all *Sharīʿa* unconfirmed by *Ḥaqīqa* is unacceptable; and all *Ḥaqīqa* unconfirmed by *Sharīʿa* is illusory. For the Book and Sunna are the origin of both *Sharīʿa* and *Ḥaqīqa*, and both are revealed knowledge that is infallible, **Error comes not to it from before nor from behind it; a sending down from one All-Wise, All-Praiseworthy**[84].

The Formidable Qur'ān is more than sufficient to solve every problem and treat every intractable illness. The Sunna explains and clarifies it to perfection, so that no rulings need come from elsewhere for those possessed of understanding, wisdom, and learning. He ﷻ says, **And We have sent down the Book upon you as a clarification of everything**[85]. And He ﷻ says, **It is not for this to be an invented tale, but a confirmation of that which was before it and a detailed explanation of everything**[86]. And He ﷻ says, **We have neglected nothing in the Book**[87].

Junayd said, 'This knowledge of ours is governed by the Book and Sunna.' Another person of authority said, 'Any understanding or opening unconfirmed by the Book and Sunna is worthless, for no saint is given openings in other than understanding the August Book and the Sunna, and his entire knowledge does not exceed them. Should it exceed them, it is neither knowledge nor unveiling, but if closely examined, will turn out to be nothing but ignorance.'[01]

Third Principle

The Science of Sufism, which is also called the Science of the Inward, has two divisions: the Science of *Raqā'iq* or 'subtle things that soften the heart', and the Science of *Ḥaqā'iq* or spiritual realities. Sufism with both its divisions can only be mastered when the outward laws are mastered and implemented, for it is their branch and their goal in this life and the Next. We do not mean studying these laws in the manner of the people of polemics, as mere words, but to receive them from the virtuous Predecessors with faith, acceptance, submission, and surrender to what is handed down, with unswerving emulation of God and the Messenger, in conformity with what they made conditional or not, in every matter, according to Revelation. The heart must be prepared by forsaking all vice and adorning itself with virtue, so that the light that descends may manifest itself through these

01 The gist of this principle is that Sufism is one of the religious sciences of Islam and is contained well within them. In fact it is their very centre, although because of its depth it is not accessible to those who have neither the desire to strive nor the required aptitude. Thus the masters may state unequivocally that everything claimed to be *Ḥaqīqa* but found to diverge from the Sacred Law is to be rejected as false.

branches upon these principles, according to the overflow, not the thinking mind. This is the fruit of fearing God at every step.

God says, and He is the most Truthful Speaker, **If you fear God, He will give you discrimination**[88]. He who fears God, He shall grant him a way out of every problem and distress, **and provide for him from whence he does not expect**[89], from ways other than sensory perception and thinking. And He says, **Is he whose breast God expands for Islam so that he is upon a light from his Lord. . .?**[90] **Is he who was dead and whom We brought to life, and made a light for him to walk by among the people. . .?**[91] There are many similar verses and even more *Ḥadīth*s. It is [a matter of] good traits of character, good taste, good demeanor, and states. The perfection of these is received through the intermediary of the people of perfection, not simply by acquisition, which is done by means of studying the sciences and accumulating the works.

First Division: The Science of *Raqā'iq* or 'subtle things that soften the heart', and of Sufism and Wayfaring (*Sulūk*).

The first division, known as *Raqā'iq*, Sufism, *Sulūk*, or Science of Transactions, is concerned with making the inward thrive with transactions of the heart, by divesting it of deleterious things and adorning it with saving ones. It is required under all circumstances and includes things that are individual obligations (*Farḍ 'Ayn*), others that are collective obligations (*Farḍ Kifāya*), and others that are recommended (*Mandūb*).

That which is an individual obligation incumbent upon every person is that upon which depends the performance of both outward and inward duties, so that one does not expose oneself to wrath, and avoids prohibited things, both apparent and hidden, in order that that no sin remain. Anything beyond that is either a collective obligation or a recommended action.

This science is the loftiest as concerns religion; it is considered to be the true *Fiqh* and the most important science by the God-fearing scholars, the people of certainty. This is because its subject is the acts of the heart and it is the means to correct and purify them from ailments and defects, and thus prepare them for the manifestation of knowledge, the secrets of the sciences, and the lights of the Unseen. There is no doubt that the acts of the heart are much more important than those of the body.

Good works are only sound when they come from a sound heart, for a *ḥadīth* says, *In the body there is a lump of flesh. When it is sound, the whole body is sound; but when it is unsound, the whole body is unsound. Truly it is the heart*[92]. Therefore, to strive to improve the heart is incumbent upon every human being, for it is what makes him human. It is the source of faith and the rising-place of spiritual stations and excellence. Thus when [that] heart is ill with distraction, then dies of hardness, and its light withers away in the shadows of rebellion, its fate becomes eternal death, permanent wrath, and utmost failure. But if the body dies from an illness of the [physical] heart, the person is in no way diminished; on the contrary, his patience may increase his degree in religion.

In sum, the benefits of this science that improves the hearts cannot be counted, nor fully detailed, nor entirely expressed, and only the experts know its true worth. It is the path to realizing the reality of religion, and acquiring the attributes of God and the God-fearing, tasting pure knowledge and unadulterated certainty. It is more comprehensive than the science of rulings, wider in scope in its branches and divisions, more precise in its meanings, and sweeter in its clarifications—but more difficult to comprehend, because the attributes of the hearts and its qualities, both praiseworthy and blameworthy, are inexhaustible. They cannot be fully apprehended as concerns their definitions and conditions, in their realities, subtleties, and profusion for certain things may be so obscure as to be inexpressible, either explicitly or implicitly, and it is then that rejection may occur, because they are so strange and unfamiliar.

This science is mostly acquired in the case of the people of certainty by means of the lights of intuition and inspiration, and in the case of the God-fearing by facing such hearts as are sound and pure from doubt, conjecture, or illusion[01].

Second Division: The Science of *Ḥaqā'iq* or spiritual realities and *Mukāshafa* or Unveiling, the *Ladunnī* (from God's Presence) or *Ilāhī* (Divine) knowledge[02] is concerned with knowledge of the Real in His

01 Here those who reach the said stage are divided into two broad categories. The first, the People of Certainty, receive their knowledge by intuition and inspiration; these the author describes as those whose hearts are sound and free from ailments. The second category, the God-fearing, reform their hearts by keeping company with the first, facing them and receiving the influx of their lights in their hearts.

02 *ʿIlm Ladunnī* means knowledge proceeding from the Presence of God. The term comes from *Sūrat al-Kahf* 18:65, where God says, **Then they found one of Our servants to whom We had given of Our mercy and taught knowledge proceeding from Us.**

Essence and Attributes, as well as knowledge of the overflow of His light and liberality on the various creatures in all their determinations, both general and particular. This comes about through knowledge, tasting, and contemplation. It is the highest science of all, their goal, their most profound center, and their ultimate end.

It is a Divine light that appears to hearts once they have been purified and cleansed from ailments, so that the realities of things become apparent, as well as the meanings of both the theoretical and the practical rulings, and how they correspond and relate to each other. It shows how to derive details from summations and taste meanings and determinations, as well as other things such as cannot be reckoned in writing, nor fully contained in breasts. Then comes direct knowledge of God, of His Essence, Attributes, and Acts, and His rulings and wisdom, in the whole universe, in its various states, secrets, and the lights that permeate the meanings within it and its changes. Thus is the veil lifted so that the clear truth is revealed as if by direct vision and the door is opened to that knowledge which requires no explanation; this is the real knowledge that fulfills every aim in comprehending existence and the overflow of light and liberality[01]. Nothing escapes this knowledge, for the people of tasting and contemplation.

This knowledge is possible for every human being, for man was created in the best of constitutions and the most upright balance. **The likeness of His Light is as a niche in which is a lamp; the lamp is in a glass, the glass is as a bright star. It is being kindled from a blessed tree, an olive that is neither of the East nor of the West, whose oil is almost alight although no fire touched it; light upon light**[93]. But upon the mirror of his heart have accumulated rust, dirt, and veils, and it has grown dark with the veils of

---

This was the knowledge of hidden things that God had granted al-Khiḍr, to allow him to see the true causes and details behind the appearance of the situations he was faced with. *'Ilm Ilāhī*, meaning Divine knowledge, is direct knowledge of God Himself in His attributes and actions.

01 The author often couples these two terms together: light and liberality. These are the two main things that overflow from the Divine Presence upon creation, sustaining it at every instant. Light is existence as opposed to nothingness, consciousness as opposed to unconsciousness, and knowledge as opposed to ignorance. Liberality refers to the liberal manner in which God showers His unceasing gifts of life, food, drink, spouse, dwelling, and so on upon creation. Both these are known of mentally by ordinary believers, but are witnessed directly by the saints.

distraction, passion, hardness, and sins, **like shadows on a dark sea, covered by waves upon which are waves, above which are clouds, shadows one on top of the other; when he extends his hand he can barely see it**[94]. Thus did God return [man] to the lowest of the low, where he becomes beneath qualifying for knowledge of the Truth, the realities, and direct knowledge. Should he then return to his Lord and ascend back to the highest level where he started[01], then in proportion to his inward purity and the brightness of the mirror of his heart and of his insight, these meanings and secrets will appear to him on the tablet of his heart.

There is no end to the lights and divisions of this noble science, nor are there limits to the details of its branches as they subdivide, for it concerns the Essence and Attributes, which are infinite. This makes it the most extensive of all sciences, since it includes all other sciences, and even anything at all that can ever be known. Its benefits are the most immense, for its subject is the knowledge of the Truth and the realities, and of every act of liberality and creation. It is also the truest, according to the testimonies of both rational and transmitted knowledge and the contemplation of the people of tasting and witnessing[02].

Fourth Principle

Some people find strange the mere existence of such a thing as this *Ladunnī* knowledge, so they deny and attack it; for they are ignorant of it, and man is the enemy of what he does not know. They treat it with contempt and confine knowledge to *Fiqh*, *Uṣūl* or Principles[03], *Ḥadīth*, and *Tafsīr*, claiming that they can find no trace of this *Ladunnī* knowledge such as is tasted by the people of *Ṭarīqa* and witnessed by the people of *Ḥaqīqa*, nor can they detect any of its effects. That is the limit of their knowledge, for they are

01 Man's starting point is when the spirits, before being sent down to Earth, are in the Divine Presence in the highest world of all.

02 The three main sources that confirm the truth of that knowledge are the intelligent mind and its rational operations, the regularly transmitted knowledge of Revelation, and the direct contemplation of Knowers.

03 *Uṣūl* means principles, or roots, or foundations. There are two sciences of principles, *Uṣūl al-Dīn*, the Principles of Religion, which is concerned with beliefs, and *Uṣūl al-Fiqh*, Principles of Jurisprudence, which is the science of the method of deriving the rulings of the Sacred Law from the sources. It teaches the art of how to use the sources to reach valid conclusions.

satisfied with less and have fallen into neglect, and only those will know its worth who have tasted and witnessed it and will then know it by experience.

Others go to the other extreme, saying that this is the true knowledge and he who has it needs no other, for it will suffice him in all his affairs, as concerns both *Sharīʿa* and *Ḥaqīqa*. The inescapable truth is that the Book and Sunna and the sciences of *Sharīʿa* are the origins, and the aforesaid knowledge is their branch and originates in them, so that it can be attained only through them and without them the goal can never be reached. This is what is meant when they say 'Knowledge is only by learning'[01], for the Book and Sunna are its bases. Thus, spiritual knowledge, perfect and noble as it is in itself, cannot allow one to dispense with the other sciences, whether of the kind that is transmitted and received, or that which is rationally deduced by intellects, secrets, and the use of insight. Following this will rivers of knowledge gush forth, according to the purification of the heart and the acuteness of understanding. It is from these principles that they will branch out, aided by the lights of perspicacity and the gifts of inspiration, and then mastery will be attained that is unblemished by conjecture and unadulterated by illusion.

He who follows the path of these people, who are truly blameless, follows in their footsteps, and is guided by their lights, will recognize this by means of tasting, unveiling, and contemplation. He will know the truth in all the realities by the overflow of the lights of liberality from the Necessary Existent.

What Imām al-Ghazālī Said Concerning Eagerness for Realities

In his book *al-Munqidh min al-Ḍalāl*, (The Savior from Error), Ghazālī explains how he had mastered the sciences that people have and reached their realities, ultimate aims, and whatever perfection it is possible to attain through them. He then says:

'Once I was done with these sciences, my will turned to the path of the Sufis. I knew that their path can be completed only by knowledge and works, so I began to acquire their knowledge and acquired all that can be attained of their knowledge by listening and learning. It then became apparent that the innermost essence of their knowledge cannot be attained in this man-

01 This is a *ḥadīth* of the Prophet ﷺ, recorded by Bayhaqī, 352; and Ṭabarānī, *Kabīr*, 929; *Awsat*, 2663.

ner, but by tasting, spiritual states, and changing one's attributes; for how much difference there is between knowing the definition of health or satiety, together with their preconditions and causes, and actually being healthy or satiated! How much difference between being drunk and merely knowing the definition of drunkenness! The one who is drunk knows nothing of the definition of drunkenness, whereas the one who is sober knows its definition and what causes it, but of drunkenness itself possesses nothing. Similarly, there is a difference between knowing the reality of detachment, its conditions and divisions, and being in actual fact inwardly detached, desiring nothing of the world.

I thus came to know with certainty that [the Sufis] are the people of states, not of words, and that whatever it was possible to acquire of their knowledge by way of learning I had already acquired. That only remained which it is not possible to acquire by listening and learning, but only by wayfaring and tasting.'

He then describes how he left Baghdad seeking this kind of wayfaring, how he entered into retreat (*Khalwa*), self-discipline (*Riyāḍa*), battling against the ego (*Mujāhada*), and seclusion (*ʿUzla*), persevering thus for ten years, after which, as he says:

'During these retreats innumerable things were unveiled to me, of which I shall only mention the following so that you can benefit from it: I learned with certainty that the Sufis are the élite of those who travel the Path to God, that their behavior is the best of all behavior, their method the best of all methods, and their character traits the best of all character traits, so that if all the intelligence of the intelligent were to be pooled together, with all the wisdom of the wise, and the knowledge of those scholars who are cognizant of the secrets of the Sacred Law, to change anything of their behavior and character, and replace it with better, they could not. For all of their movements and stillnesses, and their outwards and inwards, are derived from the niche of light of Prophethood—and there is not on Earth a better light than the Light of Prophethood to light one's way.

What can anyone say about their manner of purification, which is the first condition of their path? It is nothing less than the thorough purification of the heart from all other than God. Its key, which is for it the equivalent of formally entering into the Ritual Prayer, is that the heart be entirely immersed in the remembrance of God, while its end is complete extinction in God. This is its end in relation to what cannot be attained by choice and effort during its beginnings; but in reality it is the beginning of the path and what follows is as a corridor for the traveler[01].

From the beginning of the path they are liable to have unveilings and contemplations, so that even as they are awake they see the angels, the spirits of the Prophets, and other images, to an extent that surpasses verbal description, so anyone who tries to express them will inevitably use formulations containing obvious errors.

Generally, their journey ends up with such nearness as may induce some to imagine incarnation (*Ḥulūl*), others union (*Ittiḥād*), and others arrival (*Wuṣūl*), all which is wrong. We have explained these errors in our work *al-Maqṣad al-Asnā*[02]. Consequently, anyone who experiences such states should say no more than the following:

What happened did so, I shall say nothing;
so think well and ask not what it was.

On the whole, he who has not tasted any of this will know of the reality of Prophecy nothing but its name, for in reality, the end-point of the saints is the starting-point for Prophets.

That was the state of the Messenger of God, may God's blessings and peace be upon him, when he was worshiping in the Cave of Hirā' where he used to go into retreat and be alone with his Lord, worshiping Him, to the point that the Arabs said, 'Muḥammad is impassioned with His Lord!'

---

01 The Imām here contrasts the purification of the Sufis, which is the inward purification of the heart from bad traits, appetites, passions, and thoughts, so that it becomes occupied with nothing but the remembrance of God, with the usual outward purification (*wuḍū'*) prescribed by the Sacred Law. That the heart becomes occupied with nothing but the remembrance of God is the key to the beginning of the Path and is the equivalent of saying *Allāh Akbar* to proclaim our engagement in the ritual prayer. These practices brighten the mirror of the heart so that dream-visions, visions of the World of Similitudes, and inspirations begin to occur to the traveler; but these are all concerned with created beings and are thus far from being the real aim of the path, which is to attain to extinction in God. This, for true travelers, is in reality the first step in their path of direct knowledge, after which the path becomes clearer, just as it does for a person as they walk down a corridor and are thus able to know unequivocally in which direction to move.

02 Ghazālī's *al-Maqṣad al-asnā fi sharḥ Asmā' Allāh al-Ḥusnā*, 'The Most Brilliant Aim: a Commentary on the Most Beautiful Names of God', is a masterpiece explaining the meanings of the ninety-nine Divine Names.

This is a state that is realized by tasting for him who travels its path. He who is not granted tasting will know of it with certainty when he keeps constant company with its people, hears of their experiences, and reaches certainty in his understanding with the accumulation of evidence. Thus, he who keeps their company will benefit from them this kind of faith, for 'they are the people whose companions never suffer wretchedness[01].' As for him who is not granted to keep their company, let him have the certainty of the possibility of this, and that this certainty is achieved by means of external evidence, as we have explained in the Book of the Marvels of the Heart, in the *Iḥyā'*[02].

Thus, certainty by means of evidence is knowledge. Direct experience of this state is tasting. Accepting it by listening to the experiences of others is faith. These are three degrees. **God raises those who believe among you, and those who are given knowledge, in degrees.**[95] Beyond these are ignorant people who deny the very possibility of this and marvel at it, saying, 'How can they taste?' About them God the Exalted says, **When they leave your presence, they say to those who have been given knowledge, 'What did he just say?' Those are they whose hearts God has sealed and who follow their caprices**[96].

The evidence he mentions in the Book of the Marvels of the Heart is not far from what he explained in *Savior from Error* and other works of his.

The gist of it is that a human being when first created is naïve and simple, unaware of the innumerable worlds of God. Then his perceptual faculties are granted, so that with each of them he perceives a particular kind of things. As God says, **And God brought you out from your mothers' bellies knowing nothing, and made for you hearing and vision**[97].

The first thing that is created in man is the sense of touch, with which he perceives many kinds of things, such as heat, moisture, softness, and their opposites. But he remains ineffective in terms of smelling, eyesight, and hearing, so that things such as wind, color, and sound are for him as if inexistent. Then vision is created for him and he perceives colors and shapes, then hearing, and he perceives sounds, then taste. Then he goes beyond the world of material perception when mental discrimination is created in

---

01 See p. 27 footnote 02, See p. 79 footnote 01.

02 Ghazālī, *Iḥyā' ʿulūm al-Dīn, Kitāb ʿAjā'ib al-qalb* (the Book of the Marvels of the Heart).

him, which is another stage in his development, wherein he grasps things other than what his senses perceive. Then he is raised to another stage when intelligence is created in him, so that he grasps the difference between the necessary, the possible, and the impossible, and other things he could not grasp in previous stages.

Beyond intelligence there are two more stages: inspiration, unveiling, and true dream-visions on the one hand; and beyond that, Prophethood and Messengership. The proof that they exist is that there are in the world kinds of knowledge that cannot conceivably have been obtained either through the senses, the intelligence, or experience, such as numerous facts concerning, for example, the science of the stars, medicine, and the properties of things, as will be known by those familiar with them.

This is for those who deny Prophecy. As for those who acknowledge it, then if it is rationally possible for a Prophet to tell of unseen and future things, it is equally possible for other created beings to perceive them. Also, true dream-visions reveal the Unseen, and if this is possible during sleep then it is not impossible in the waking state, for being asleep and awake differ only in the inactivity of the senses during the first, when they are not being occupied with material things. Similarly, a person may ostensibly be awake, yet be so preoccupied that he neither hears, nor sees.

Now just as we know for sure that different kinds of sensory perceptions are distinct from each other, and sensory perception as such is distinct from mental discrimination, which in turn is distinct from all that is grasped by the intelligence, so is the intelligence distinct from what lies beyond it in the way of inspiration and revelation.

When the operations of the intelligence are brought to the notice of the possessor of mental discrimination, he denies and thinks them far-fetched. Similarly, some intelligent people deny and think far-fetched inspiration and revelation. This is sheer ignorance, for they are basing their attitude on nothing more than that this is a stage they have yet to reach, and therefore consider inexistent. If someone who is born blind never hears frequent descriptions of colors and shapes, then is suddenly told about them, he will not understand, nor will he be able to conceive of them. Anyone who knows about dream-visions and knows that the sleeper, although akin to a dead person or a log, nevertheless perceives certain unseen things, either explicitly or as symbols, will have to acknowledge this. Similarly, anyone who acknowledges Prophecy also acknowledges this.

God graciously grants dream-visions and He has made them a model for [one of the attributes of] Prophecy, so that intelligent people may acknowledge it, for he who knows no model for a thing will neither understand nor acknowledge it. This, however, is only one of the attributes of Prophecy; as for higher ones, they are grasped only by tasting, by traveling the Sufi path. In his beginnings on the Sufi Path, the traveler may experience some of these and attain to some tasting according to his capacity, which will lead him to believe in the rest that he has not experienced.'

This is similar to what Imām al-Ghazālī said before, which is that he who has not been given to taste any of these things will know nothing of the reality of Prophecy but its name. He also says in *Mishkāt al-anwār*, The Niche of Lights:

'There are some kinds of Divine knowledge that are beyond the powers of the intellectual rational spirit. He who is confined to the world of intelligence cannot deny the stage beyond it where things appear which do not appear to the intelligence, just as it is possible for the intelligence to be a stage beyond mental discrimination and sensory perception, where appear worlds and marvels that such perception falls short of.

'It has been said, 'The limits of the thinking mind include all that can be rationally grasped, inasmuch as the mind thinks, but not inasmuch as it is receptive and capable of freeing itself from being limited by thinking. Minds that are limited by their thoughts may decide that many things are impossible that, in other minds that are sound and free of the said limits, are not only possible but inevitable. Free minds stop at no limits inasmuch as they are receptive; on the contrary, they are always rising to higher stations and receiving input from unseen sources and the Divine Presences. **Whatever mercy God opens for people none can withhold, and whatever He withholds none can release after Him.**[98]'

A Comment on the Difference between the Imagination and the Intelligence

Sensory perception and the imagination may decide upon things that the intelligence does not accept. An example is sensory perception deciding that the shadow of a thing is static[01]; another is the imagination clothing meanings in images; yet another is to attribute color and taste to the

01 A shadow, being dependent on the sun's position altering with the rotation of the earth, can never be still, even for a split second, yet the eye perceives it as quite still.

scent of musk. These are all things that pure intelligence judges incorrect; nevertheless, they may still confound it to a certain extent. They may even overcome a weak intelligence so that it fears any black thing at night, or something far away before identifying it, imagining it to be dangerous, or something it well knows but hears a poet describing as evil; or fear honey, having heard someone say it causes nausea and vomiting, or is bitter. The reason is that human beings are more comfortable with their senses and imagination, since those were created before the controlling intelligence.

Similarly, if the controlling intelligence is accustomed to receive its input from the senses and its own thoughts, and believes that there can be no knowledge except that which is learned in this manner, and nothing beyond that, it will be a prisoner of the world of forms, shackled by its thoughts, and thereby prevented from receiving what comes from higher up. You will thus find that the intelligence that is tied up by thoughts and attached to sensory perception, imaginations, and illusion, will consider impossible what the Prophet who is sent with the tongue of his people, the people of God, conveys to them about the anthropomorphic Names and Attributes of God. For those whose intelligence is limited by their thoughts and overcome by their imagination are driven to interpret these in such a manner as to make them miss both the perfection of faith and the perfection of knowledge. Now even if the interpretation be correct, it does not become knowledge, for it shall always remain [merely] probable; what, then, when error in this is more likely than not?

The Obligation to Accept the Beliefs of the Virtuous Predecessors

It is incumbent upon him who is possessed of religious determination and seeks gifts of certitude from the Presence of God, to purify his heart from base character traits and worldly desires, transcend with his innermost core all ordinary limits, contingencies and worldly events, and start from his very beginning with the creed of his virtuous Predecessors. Those are they who believe in God and His Messenger and follow them in what they say and everything that was revealed. Thus are they safe from the shackles of intelligence and reasoning, which lead to resorting to similitudes (*Tamthīl*), anthropomorphism (*Tashbīh*), neutralization (*Taʿṭīl*), or interpretation (*Ta'wīl*) using an intelligence that is too limited to attain the realization of transcendence. Thus does belief become adulterated with conjecture, which may introduce heresy (*Bidʿa*). One should therefore believe in the ambiguous verses, and the Names and Attributes, in the manner they were formulated, and attribute them to God as He wishes them to be, together with the attribution of Transcendence. **There is nothing like Him**[99]. He is not as the people of interpretation describe Him, using mere mental conjecture; for they may perceive something as an attribute of perfection that is worthy of the Real, whereas in the knowledge of the Real ﷻ, it is an imperfection; and vice versa.

This is because the knowledge of God as given by the Sacred Law, joining apparently ambiguous descriptions with the attribution of Transcendence, **There is nothing like Him,** is beyond the capacity of intelligence inasmuch as it thinks, but not inasmuch as it is capable of receiving Divine gifts. Al-Shāfiʿī has said, 'Intelligence has a limit where it stops, just as eyesight has a limit where it stops.'

And God knows best.

If you ask, 'How can there be a power above the power of intelligence, when the Messenger of God was sent to those endowed with intelligence, for it is to intelligence, the presence of which is the precondition of legal responsibility, that the Sacred Law is addressed?' I would answer, 'The address to those endowed with intelligence is one requiring faith and acceptance; and intelligence is capable of that, even if it does not grasp its reality. Such persons will thus believe in following God and His Messenger, then, as they rise in the degrees of religion and God-fearing, and the eye of insight and certainty opens, will taste all this by direct experience and grasp it by contemplation and vision. And just as they are charged first of all with the two Testimonies in sum, followed by what is immediately required in terms of works, and requires details only as situations unfold, so here they are first to follow God and His Messenger, then subsequently taste and know, and rise in the degrees of perfection. And just as necessary obvious information occurs in the heart without external cause, but by being a Divine gift then multiplies and become food for thought in addition to the information acquired by the senses and rational operations, so does God grant those He will of His saints knowledge from His Presence (*Ladunnī*), and to His Prophets Revelation. This knowledge grows and diversifies by the remembrance of God and His Attributes, and reflection on what He revealed in His Book and the *Sunna* of His Messenger. This will be recognized by those who have practiced and experienced it.

Fifth Principle

This is about the evidence for the existence of this knowledge within handed-down knowledge, verses and *Ḥadīth*s, and information from the Predecessors, and that it is beyond the power of intelligence and known only to its adepts, and only to them is it permissible to divulge its secrets, for they are the people whose superiority is unblemished by imperfection.

God the Exalted says, **We have left nothing out of the Book**[100]. And He ﷻ says, **This is no invented tale, but a confirmation of what came before and a detailed explanation of everything**[101]. And He says, **There is nothing, moist or dry, but is in a clear book**[102].

And he ﷺ said, *The Qur'ān was sent down according to seven readings, each of which has an outward and an inward; each inward has a limit, and each limit a rising-place*[01]. And in another version, *Each verse has an outward and an inward, and each inward has another inward, to seven inwards*[02].

Ibn ʿAbbās said, 'The Qur'ān is made of sudden shifts from one subject to another, artful expressions, outwards, and inwards. Its wonders are never exhausted and its limit never reached.' Ibn Masʿūd said, 'Whoever desires the knowledge of the ancients and the latecomers, let him meditate on the Qur'ān.' And ʿAlī, may God be pleased with him, said, 'Had I wished to load seventy camels with one verse of the Qur'ān, I could have done.' And in another version, 'with the *Basmala*', and in yet another, 'forty camels with the *Fātiha*.' And when he was asked, may God be pleased with him, whether the Messenger of God had given them [his immediate family, the People of the House) something exclusive, he said in the course of his reply, 'or understanding that a man is given in the Book of God.' And the Prophet ﷺ prayed, for Ibn ʿAbbās, 'O God, give him understanding of the religion and teach him interpretation.' This is why Ibn ʿAbbās is reported to have said concerning the ambiguous verses, 'I am among those who know their interpretation.' He is also reported to have said, 'The interpretation of the ambiguous is known only to God, and anyone who claims otherwise is a liar.' To harmonize both statements: what which is affirmed is knowledge of it via Divine grace in the manner of **And He taught you that which you**

01 *The Qur'ān was sent down according to seven readings*. This part of the *ḥadīth* is in Bukhārī, *Ṣaḥīḥ*, 241: in full it is in Ṭabarī, *Tafsīr*, 1:22; Abū Yaʿlā, *Musnad*, 5149.

02 Shihāb al-Dīn al-Khafājī, *Ḥāshiyat al-Shihāb ʿalā Tafsīr al-Bayḍāwī*, 2:29.

did not know[103]; what is denied is knowledge [gained] through studying, for it is beyond the capacity of intelligence in its rational aspect.

These verses, *Ḥadīth*s, and other traditions indicate that *Ladunnī* knowledge is taken from the Book of God and Sunna of His Messenger, and depends on them. You may perhaps think that the better known exegeses or *tafsīrs* are sufficient or that the familiar commentaries are the ultimate in its understanding, but what scholar has ever given it its due in exegesis, and what commentator has ever fully discharged his responsibility? Every exegete has commented from one point of view, according to his capacity and understanding. They have never exhausted it; it is still fresh and tender, with oceans of sciences gushing forth from every word of it every day, according to qualification and comprehension.

If its outward expressions have defeated the masters of all eloquence and the bastions of pure language, how much more will its meanings astound them!

I have seen how a contemporary scholar declared that grammatical analysis of the passage **Alif, Lām, Mīm. That is the Book, no doubt about it, a guidance for the God-fearing**[104] is capable of being multiplied so as to reach the number made by single digits: 987654321—that is, nine hundred and eighty seven million, six hundred and fifty four thousand, three hundred and twenty one. He gave the details for one long sentence [as an example] and alluded to the rest. The meanings will inevitably vary with the variations in grammatical analysis and will increase to infinity. Transcendent is the Subtle, the All-Aware!

How can its wonders ever be exhausted or its marvels ever end, when it is the Word of God and is one of His Attributes, which are limitless in themselves and infinite in their relationships? Only He who spoke it knows its secrets.

Similarly the Sunna of His Prophet ﷺ, who was given 'comprehensiveness of speech', **He speaks not out from caprice. It is but revelation that is revealed**[105] for it is inseparable from the Qur'ān; they both come from the same niche. The realities of their meanings and the subtleties they contain appear only **to one who listens and is watchful**[106], who has divested himself of all attachments while following the Straight Path, and renounced all obstacles when tasting the secrets of *Tawḥīd*. He has purified his heart, and sanctified his core, so that the mirror of his heart, by the light of

Prophethood and the secret of chivalry (*futuwwa*)[01], has become polished. Otherwise his understanding will remain confined to the outward form of the expressions and fall short of grasping the subtle meaning and allusions. This is where from the Book and Sunna shall knowledge and science be caused to gush forth for the people of secrets, and by the Divine Light shall be unveiled for them the realities and subtleties which if heard about by others will be denied, criticized, and declared false and having to be changed. This is because he who has never tasted its sweetness, owing to the bitterness in his own mouth, does not recognize it owing to the imperfection of his own knowledge and understanding.

The Various States of People with Regard to the Science of Realities

How often have certain people been impelled by their own ignorance to declare its people ignorant and accuse them of religious monstrosities, because its meanings are difficult to express and suggest at first sight unacceptable things such as imagining that the utterance indicates incarnation or union, or transgresses the limits of the Sacred Law and the rightly-guided Path! They are innocent of all this, however, and far from them be it, for they are the leaders, the Knowers, the scholars of authority, and the God-fearing saints. But those who deny do so just like the ancients denied when they said, 'A sorcerer or madman!' These have exceedingly deficient. . . . . .

Others overshoot the limits of what is correct, and fall into excess and confusion. They are deceived by this noble science, fall into contradicting the Sacred Law, cast off their legal responsibility, fall into the most extreme errors, believe in incarnation and union, incline to immorality and atheism, and depart from the circle of the rightly-guided.

Some scholars are of the opinion that it is not permitted to read this science, or spread it, and that discussing it is forbidden, even with its people, for fear of this confounding fumbling leading religious people into temp-

---

01 *Futuwwa* is gallantry, chivalry, manliness, magnanimity, and generosity all together. The *Fatā* is one who embodies all those qualities and is thus the epitome of virile nobility. There is usually a chapter on *Futuwwa* in Sufi treatises. Apart from the Sufis' insistence on *Futuwwa* as a vital attribute to be acquired by disciples, there used to be non-Sufi *Futuwwa* brotherhoods, whose members were pledged to give generous hospitality to strangers and passers-by, help the needy, and save those in distress, all for the sake of God.

tation. The inescapable truth is that this differs for different people. For him who would suffer harm in his religion and whose beliefs and certainty would be shaken, it is forbidden. As for him who recognizes it when he hears it from its people and tastes the realization of its details by connecting its branches to its principles, it is one of the best of all sciences. There is nothing strange in this, for the sun benefits most people but harms the eyes of many animals. There is no harm in reading these books for him who thinks well of its people and is not critical of them, and who will either benefit or [when he does not understand] accept that what the intention behind their words is sound.

The words of the Predecessors should be understood in this manner. The sciences of secrets are beyond the limits of intelligence and rational thinking, and the more they are explained the stranger they appear. They are thus ungraspable to weak minds, the minds of those who are all too permeated with *bidʿa*, suffer from vices such as *kibr* (arrogance or conceit), and believe that there can be no knowledge save through ordinary learning. This is why anyone who wishes to explain this science to those unqualified can only do so by way of allusions, examples, and poetry—and on condition that he has mastery of the other sciences as well.

Leading scholars, but also others, have always conceded to the People that which they fail to understand; they do not deny it. It is reported that Imām Abū al-ʿAbbās Ibn Surayj[01] once attended a [teaching] session with Junayd, after which he was asked, 'Did you understand what he said?' He answered, 'I do not know what he said, but I found a manifest effect on my heart, indicating outward works and inward sincerity.'

It is reported that Abū Hurayra, may God be pleased with him, said, 'I received from the Messenger of God ﷺ, two receptacles. One of them I disseminated among people; as for the other, should I disseminate it, this gullet of mine would be cut!' He meant his oesophagus.

Ghazālī says in the *Iḥyā'*, 'This is the science that is not to be written in books, nor discussed by their adepts, except in private, and with those who are qualified, who participate in it by listening. This hidden science is that meant by the Prophet ﷺ, when he said, *Some knowledge is hidden, known only to those who know God; when they speak about it, it is misunderstood only*

---

01 Imām Abū al-ʿAbbās Ibn Surayj of Baghdad (d. 306/918) was a master of Shāfiʿī jurisprudence and a transmitter of *ḥadīth*s.

by those who have illusions about God[01]. Therefore, never despise a learned man to whom God has given knowledge, for He was not despising him when He gave it to him.'

Ibn ʿAbbās, may God be pleased with him and his father, is reported to have said, 'Were I to tell you what I know of the meaning of His ﷻ saying, **And the matter descends between them,**[107] you would stone me, claiming I am a disbeliever!'

Ghazālī quotes the following verses of Imām Zayn al-ʿĀbidīn, ʿAlī ibn al-Ḥusayn—may God be pleased with him and his father:

Of my knowledge I hide the jewels
from the ignorant lest they stray.
Abū al-Ḥasan did this before by
who enjoined it upon Ḥusayn and Ḥasan.
For should its essence be divulged
they will accuse me of idolatry.
Muslims will think it lawful to kill me
applauding this most villainous deed.

Says Ghazālī, 'He meant knowledge which would make them consider shedding his blood permissible—the sciences of secrets and *Ladunnī* knowledge—not, as some have claimed, knowledge of who will be enthroned as Caliph and who will be deposed. This latter kind would not lead Muslim scholars to consider shedding his blood permitted, nor to accuse him of idolatry.'

Sahl ibn ʿAbd Allāh[02] said, 'After the year 300 it will no longer be permitted to speak of this knowledge of ours.'

Shaykh Abū ʿAbd Allāh al-Qurashī[03] said, 'It has been forty years since I could find anyone to talk of realities with. I am so worried that I will lose this knowledge that I lie down and talk about it to myself.'

It is reported that al-Ḥasan al-Baṣrī, al-Junayd, al-Shiblī[04], and those

---

01 Daylamī, *Musnad al-Firdaws*, 802; Abū ʿAbd al-Raḥmān al-Sulamī, *al-Arbaʿūn fi al-ṭaṣawwuf*, 32.

02 Sahl ibn ʿAbd Allāh al-Tustarī, famous Sufi and author who was born in Tustar, near Shiraz in Iran and died in Baṣra in 283/869.

03 Abū ʿAbd Allāh ibn Aḥmad al-Qurashī was a famous Sufi from Iraq who lived for a long time in Egypt and died in 599/1203.

04 Abū Bakr al-Shiblī was a famous Sufi who was Imām al-Junayd's disciple and became

like them never discussed the sciences of *Tawḥīd* save in the depths of their houses, having hidden the keys under their thighs. They answered those who blamed them by saying, 'Do you wish God and His Messenger to be given the lie, or the Companions and Followers from whom we have taken this knowledge to be unjustly and unjustifiably accused of disbelief and heresy?'

This attitude is confirmed by his ﷺ saying, *Talk to people according to their intelligence*[01]. And, *Talk to people according to what they know; do you wish God and His Messenger to be given the lie?*[02] And, *We Prophets are ordered to treat people according to their ranks and talk to them according to their intelligence*[03]. And, *None shall ever talk to a group of people about things beyond their intelligence but that it will be a temptation for some of them.*[04]

And ʿAlī pointed to his chest, saying, 'There are abundant sciences in here, if only they could find someone to carry them.' He spoke truly, for 'The hearts of the righteous are the tombs of secrets.' A certain Knower once said, 'He who divulges a secret of God these days will have lost himself and his religion, and the least of his punishments is to be deprived and tested.' Another authority used to say, 'Those who do not belong to our Path are forbidden to look into our books; and our words should be conveyed only to those who believe in them, otherwise both he who conveys and he who hears will fall into the hell of denial.' Another has said, 'He who transgresses the limits of the People and divulges the hidden secret will have deserved to be killed and censured. This is because he who transmits their words to the unqualified is like him who takes the Qurʾān to the land of an enemy who does not believe in it and will make it an object of mockery, jest, denial, and disbelief.'

Imām al-Shāfiʿī has said,

> *To give knowledge to the ignorant is to waste it,*
> *and to withhold it from the deserving is iniquitous.*

It is mostly in the science of *ḥaqāʾiq* that one comes across extravagant elocutions and unclear language, and not so much in the science of *Raqāʾiq*, for it is easier to grasp and capable of being learned in the usual way. However,

---

his successor. He was known for his ecstatic states. He died in Baghdad in 334/946.

01 Daylamī, *Musnad al-Firdaws*, 1608.

02 This was said by ʿAlī ibn Abī Ṭālib ◈. [Bukhārī, *Ṣaḥīḥ*, 127]

03 Ghazālī, *Iḥyāʾ ʿulūm al-Dīn*, 1:57.

04 This was said by the Companion ʿAbd Allāh ibn Masʿūd ◈.

. . .[01], the science of *Tawḥīd* and the utterances of the people of spiritual states and openings. Here the subtleties are too difficult to express and hard to understand, save for those well versed in this science.

Reading the books of this kind of knowledge, teaching them, and repeatedly going over them are a light for those who love the People and are loved by them, which will illuminate their hearts and cleanse their defects. Talking about them and mentioning their discourses brings about the descent of Mercy and opens up the door for the lights of the Unseen.

A certain Knower has said, 'Today nothing is more beneficial for the heart than the discourses of the People. He who persistently reads their books, learns their stories, and talks of their states, God will open the eye of his heart and expand his breast.' Another said, 'If you have missed actually meeting the saints and the great ones, then you will find in their discourses the purification of the inward and the light of insight.' And another said, 'The words of the masters are the keys for hearts.' Yet another said, 'They sometimes utter something that then remains priceless until Resurrection Day.'

Shaykh Aḥmad al-Rifāʿī[02] said, 'Learn the sciences of the Sufis, for the attraction of the Real has diminished these days.' What he meant by diminution in attraction—but God knows best—is that preparation and exposure to receive it has diminished, not that the attraction has diminished in itself.

Someone has said, 'Read the books of the Sufis, for their secrets are in their books, so that if someone reads them and seeks their lights is as if he has kept company with them and taken of their breaths.'

Abū Madyan said,

When shall I see them? How can I?
When shall [my] ear hear of their states?

Another Knower has said, 'He who occupies himself with reading the books of the People will become detached, his intentions will improve, his works will become more gracious, and he will distance himself from the

01 Some words are missing at this point.

02 Shaykh Aḥmad al-Rifāʿī, a descendant of Imām Ḥusayn, was a great Sufi master and the founder of the Rifāʿī Order which is still very widespread today. He lived in the village of Umm ʿUbayda in southern Iraq and died in 578/1182.

appetites of his soul. He will love and catch up with [the Sufis], acquiring their character and taste as they do.' Another has said, 'The Sufis are those who know God and are preoccupied with Him. They are the followers of God's Messenger and the heirs of his knowledge and state. How excellent is delving in depth into their sciences, for reading them, perusing them, studying their books, and discussing them are among the best aspects of religion and greatest causes of certainty! Mere belief in their knowledge is already sainthood, as Junayd said.

But he who shuns their sciences and turns away from their path is in danger of dying while unknowingly persisting in major sins. The terms *Fiqh* and *'Ilm* were used by the first generations to indicate only this kind of knowledge, the path to the hereafter.

Shaykh Jalāl al-Dīn al-Suyūṭī[01] said, 'Know that were the meanings of the subtleties of the sciences of Sufism to be explained to jurists using the same expressions they are accustomed to in their sciences, they would approve of them unreservedly and become their foremost proponents. What drives them away is that the said sciences are expressed in alien and disconcerting terms that they are not used to. This is why some have said that *Ḥaqīqa* is the best thing to be known and the worst to be spoken about.'

To give an example to show how true this can be: Shaykh al-Harawī says in *Manāzil al-sā'irīn*[02], 'The reality of repentance is to be ever repenting from repentance.' A jurist who hears this 'repenting from repentance' finds it very strange and asks, 'How do you repent from repentance, when repentance is a good deed? One repents from sins.' But the meaning is that when the servant becomes perfected in his return to God, he no longer gives any consideration to his works and his heart does not find peace in them,

---

01 Imām Jalāl al-Dīn al-Suyūṭī was a master of almost every religious and auxiliary science. He authored a large number of important works, including more than a commentary on the Qur'ān and compilations of *ḥadīth*s, as well as works of jurisprudence, history, biographies of generations of scholars, and collections of legal opinions on a vast number of subjects. He lived in Cairo where he died and was buried in 911/1505.

02 The author meant here is Shaykh Abū Ismā'īl 'Abd Allāh ibn Muḥammad al-Anṣārī al-Harawī who, as his name indicates, lived at Herat in Afghanistan, where he died in 481/1089. *Manāzil al-sā'irīn ilā Allāh* (The Halting-Places of the Travelers to God) is a famous treatise by Shaykh al-Anṣārī on the stages of the Path. His Persian work on the same subject, *Ṣad maydān*, has been translated into English: *Stations of the Path: the One Hundred Fields* (Sad maydan) *of Abdullah Ansari of Herat*, tr. N. Angha (Bartlow, UK, 2010).

whether they are devotional or otherwise, so that he must repent from his finding peace in his repentance. To explain further: Repentance, though an action of the servant, is created by God and He grants the success to achieve it, so that in reality He is the one who relents toward the servant and should He not do so, the servant would never repent. He ﷻ says, **Then He relented toward them, that they might repent.**[108] What part, then, does the servant play in repentance or other acts, which occur only when God creates them and grants the servant success in doing them? Thus when the servant observes his own repentance and considers it something that he has done, this is a sin that he must ask forgiveness for. He must, on the contrary, see that everything is entirely a gift from God and success granted by Him. Then the servant has to forsake any regard for himself; and this is the station of extinction in repentance, which is the first halting-place of the travelers. In the same manner should the station of extinction be witnessed at every other halting-place[01].

Now if this is explained to the jurist in such terms as these, which are terms that he is familiar with, he will be the first to approve, because jurists accept that acts are created by God, are due to His granting success, and are not the servant's creation.'

Some expressions are more comprehensive than others and some allusions clearer than others, and the discourse and argumentation should be according to the recipient's capacities. This is as far as the Science of *Raqā'iq* is concerned.

As for *Ḥaqā'iq*, discourse can be beneficial only when addressed to one who already has good knowledge of them, which means someone who has tasted, experienced, and believed. Thus only someone who believes in the People, whose heart is clear toward them, and who is their friend should be addressed with such knowledge, so that what he has not himself tasted and known he will concede and believe. If he does not believe, at least he will not deny.

A certain authority has said, 'Those who are qualified to benefit from the results of sound experiences and the sciences of unveiling are those who love and believe in the Men of God and His élite, who believe in them

---

01 The halting-places meant here are the stations of the spiritual Path, such as hope, fear, detachment, and reliance. Extinction is the final stage of each station and heralds its successful completion.

and their utterances, whose hearts are illuminated and whose natures are sound, and whose understanding is amply sufficient. **Those who call upon their Lord morning and evening, desiring His Face**[109]; **those who listen to discourse and follow the best of it**[110] with a pure mind, concentration, and attentive listening, who have cleaned their hearts of the attributes of those given to argumentation and quarreling. They will thus expose themselves, on the path of emulation, to the gifts of liberality of the Real, which God grants them from His August Presence, by whatever means to whichever degree of the degrees of His Names [He wills], either through an intermediary they know or without. They will receive it with courtesy, weighing it with the scales of common sense on some occasions and those of the élite at others, but never with the scales of sensory perception, intelligence, or rational thinking. Such a believer, whose faith and nature are sound, and whose heart is clean, gauges intuitively the truth of what he hears, through a thin veil imposed by human nature. He will reject attachments and distractions that occupy the heart and prevent him from thorough reception of the said intuition, and is thus prepared for unveiling and qualified to strive. He will benefit from what he hears, and rise with the light of faith to the degree of vision.'

There is no harm for one who is granted providential success, and is able to picture and understand the discourse of the People and believe it, repeatedly to read books such as those of Muḥyī al-Dīn Ibn ʿArabī[01], al-Jīlānī[02], Ibn al-Fāriḍ[03], and others, in the manner that they should. This is how one

01 Shaykh Muḥyī al-Dīn Ibn al-ʿArabī was a great Sufi and prolific writer from Muslim Spain who travelled much and spent the last years of his life in Damascus where he died and was buried in 638/1240. He reveals so many of the secrets of the people of unveiling in his works and they contain so many arcane and controversial points that he was considered by some scholars to have strayed outside the pale of Islam, while the majority of Sufis call him *al-Shaykh al-Akbar*, the Greatest Master.

02 The Jīlānī in question here is probably Shaykh ʿAbd al-Karīm al-Jīlānī, better known as al-Jīlī (Jīlānī and Jīlī being equivalent) of Zabīd in Northern Yemen, a student of Shaykh Ismāʿīl al-Jabartī and a prolific writer of Sufi works, the best known being *al-Insān al-Kāmil*, the Perfect Man. He died in 832/1428.

03 Shaykh ʿUmar Ibn al-Fāriḍ was a great Sufi poet who lived in Cairo. His poems spread far and wide and are still among the most frequently sung in Sufi gatherings to this day. He is often called Sulṭān al-ʿĀshiqīn, or 'Monarch of the Lovers'. Ibn al-Fāriḍ was a Knower of the highest order who revealed some of his secret knowledge in his poetry, thus causing controversy among scholars. He died in 632/1235.

should understand the words of those who encourage their reading, such as Shaykh Ismāʿīl al-Jabartī, who is said to have told one of his followers to read the books of Ibn ʿArabī, and when the student answered, 'I want to wait until I receive it from God opening the overflow,' he said, 'That which you wish to know is that which the Shaykh tells you in these books.'

Another authority said, 'A person may attain, through perusing the books of the People and understanding a single one of their concepts, that which he would attain only after fifty years of striving; for each traveler achieves the result of his own traveling and works according to his own capacity, whereas the sciences that perfected men write about are the results of their own traveling and works. For this is a Divine overflow upon their hearts according to their capacity to receive and the amplitude of their receptacles, and so is not available to those who come after them. Thus when the seeker understands what they say about a particular matter, he becomes their equal in that matter.

He who adds to what he learns from the books of the people of *Ḥaqā'iq* the virtue of traveling and striving on the path will perfect himself, and will follow and join the Knowers.

The books of the people of realities offer the science of *Tawḥīd* explicitly expressed, and the reality of *Tawḥīd* implicitly alluded to. Reading these books and working accordingly leads to the Knowledge of Certainty, followed by the Eye of Certainty, after which they are no longer of any use, for the Truth of Certainty cannot be obtained by means of books, being something that is beyond secondary means.'

Shaykh Ismāʿīl al-Jabartī also said, 'He who is given understanding of this science by God has been given a boon, for only he who has light in him can understand it.' And he said, 'Were people to study this inward knowledge as they study outward knowledge, it would imprint itself on them.'

Shaykh Dāwūd al-Shādhilī[01] said, 'Do listen to fresh news, news that is not the result of thinking or deliberation, for it benefits the heart and drives away the harm of distraction.'

A Knower once said, 'Only he understands what we say in whom has dawned the light of the Subject of our discourse.'

Whenever Shaykh Abū Madyan heard any of his followers repeat

---

01 Shaykh Abū Sulaymān Dāwūd al-Shādhilī was a 9th/15th century Mālikī jurist and Sufi Shaykh of the Shādhilī Order.

someone else's statements, he exclaimed, 'Will you not feed us God?' He wished thereby to raise his followers' aspirations and he meant, 'Give us only the fresh openings that God has opened for you in His discourse and that of His Messenger.'

Said Shaykh Muḥyī al-Dīn Ibn al- ʿArabī, 'Among the strangest things in this path, which is found nowhere else, is that when the sincere disciple enters their Path, knowing nothing at all of their language, then sits with them and hears their allusions, he understands everything they say without explanation on their part, or definition of their terms—contrary to other kinds of learning, whose terminology the student understands only after explanation. As for the terms of the people of this Path, the sincere disciple understands them all and tastes them without being taught, as if he had himself invented those terms. He discusses the knowledge with them and does not see this as unusual, but finds this knowledge imperatively self-evident within himself, as if he had always known it, and he does not know how it came about. Such is the state of the sincere disciple. As for the insincere one, he will understand only after explanation, never by mere listening, since his sincerity in the quest is deficient.'

Some who have reached the approaches of this knowledge, but without actually tasting it, may sometimes talk about it, and be led thereby to think that they have attained to it when in reality they have not.

A certain authority has said, 'Someone may talk of a station that he is drawing near to but has not actually attained. This may confuse those who are lacking in insight and inward illumination. It is like the state of someone who is striking fire. Whenever he strikes there is fire, but if he stops it dies out. He also needs to have something in which to carry the fire with him, otherwise he will lose it, although he has actually seen it. The one who is granted success must wait until he is certain, and not claim what is not really his, for thereby he would forfeit what comes after and what he has yet to attain.'

Sixth Principle

This is the explanation of the meaning of the descent of these sciences into the heart and their relation to the sciences of unveiling the unseen by means of true dream-visions and inspiration; and that what occurs to the saints is a derivative of what occurs to the Prophets, and opposes it in neither principle nor branch. Should it ever oppose it, however, then it is not true. And [an explanation] that saints will never reach the degree of Prophets, for what saints are given is inspiration, even if it be in essence like [revelation]. Such things when they occur to Prophets are for them the same as revelation[01], as in the story of al-Khalīl (the dear Friend) and his son who was to be slaughtered [i.e. Abraham and Ishmael], the story of al-Khiḍr who said **I did it not of my own volition**[111], and other stories of like significance.

It is related that *Sūrat al-Kawthar* was revealed on such an occasion, as in Muslim's *Ṣaḥīḥ*, although some have chosen to interpret it[02]. This is because Prophets have such utterly pure hearts and such powerful lights in their secrets that things are unveiled for them so clearly that no veil or confusion remains; and because of their immunity from error the Devil cannot confuse them or introduce anything into their revelations.

Nevertheless, that which saints are given resembles that which Prophets are given, as confirmed by his ﷺ saying, *Dream-visions are one part of Prophecy*[03]. And if the dream-vision is part of Prophecy then inspiration is even more so. A *ḥadīth* says, *A good dream-vision is the servant's conversation with his Lord*[04]. And God the Exalted says, **By the soul and That which shaped it, and inspired it to corruption or piety**[112]. And He ﷻ says, **Upon those who say 'Our Lord is God,' then are upright, the angels descend: 'Be not afraid, nor grieve, and rejoice in the Garden...'**[113] And He ﷻ says, **Theirs is good news in the life of this world**[114]. And He ﷻ says, **When God said to the angels, 'I am with you...'**[115]

And he said ﷺ, *There are in my Community* muḥaddathūn (those who are spoken to), Abdāl (Substitutes)[05]—and in another version, mukallamūn, also

---

01 The things in question here are dream-visions and inspiration, both of which are considered to be revelations when they occur to Prophets, but not when they occur to saints.

02 The author means that according to the story related by Anas ؓ, and recorded by Muslim in his *Ṣaḥīḥ* (400), *Sūrat al-Kawthar* was revealed in a dream-vision. Anas said, 'As the Prophet ﷺ, was sitting with us one day he fell into a brief slumber, then raised his head, smiling, and said, *A* sūra *has just been revealed to me*.' Then he recited *Sūrat al-Kawthar*, and he explained that *al-Kawthar* was a river that God had promised him and that would fill his Basin on Judgment Day.

03 Muslim, *Ṣaḥīḥ*, 2263: *The dream-vision of the believer is one of forty-six parts of Prophecy*.

04 Ibn Abī ʿĀṣim, *al-Sunna*, 486; al-Ḥakīm al-Tirmidhī, *Nawādir al-uṣūl*, 1:390; Maqdisī, *al-Aḥādīth al-mukhtāra*, 337.

05 These are parts of two separate *Ḥadīth*s, combined here to indicate the fact that

meaning those spoken to. And in a third *ḥadīth*, *There were muḥaddathūn in previous Communities, and if there be any in mine, it will be ʿUmar*[116]. His saying, *'and if there be any'* is not to make it conditional or doubtful, for his Community is the best, as he declared unequivocally, but to emphasize it, as for example, 'If I have worked for you, then give me my due!' There are different opinions as to the meaning of *muḥaddath*, but the majority understand it as one who receives inspiration, something from the Supreme Assembly that is cast into the consciousness of a sincere man and which he recognizes as spoken by other than himself. It was also said that the angels will talk to him without him being a Prophet. The intended meaning here is that they will speak to him inwardly. It has also been said that he will always speak the truth, as ʿUmar said, 'I concurred with my Lord[01].'

Anything that is possible for Prophets to receive as revelation, either through the Angel, or by insufflation into the heart, or otherwise, will be possible for the saints as a *karāma*, due to their following the Prophet. However, what comes to the Prophets is exceedingly clear and limpid, whereas what comes to others does not reach the same degree or even come close to it, even though their breasts are illuminated and their hearts find their peace in it.

Just as it is known beyond doubt that devils cast into dark hearts insinuations, imaginary things, and false dreams, so do angels cast into pure, holy, illuminated hearts sciences and understanding, and true dreams, which confirm faith, strengthen certainty, and bring about more clarity and lucidity.

What nowadays occurs to the saints confirms what has occurred in the past to the Prophets and is a witness to it. It is not nullified by the fact that the Prophet ﷺ, is the Seal of Prophethood and that after his death there are to be no more Prophets, for what has departed with him is that which is the exclusive prerogative of Prophets, which is true revelation such as brings about a Sacred Law and other rulings. This is different from inspiration, which can bring about nothing of the sort; for it never reaches the degree of true revelation such as is obligatory for all people to follow, and this is why it never takes precedence over the Sacred Law, but on the contrary, is

---

people who receive clear inspiration are frequently also *Abdāl*.

01 On several occasions ʿUmar ﷺ, is known to have said things or given his opinion on something or other, following which revelation came to the Prophet ﷺ in agreement with what ʿUmar had said and sometimes in the very same words he had used. Scholars call these *Muwāfaqāt ʿUmar* (ʿUmar's Agreements).

always secondary to it. True inspiration must conform to the Law, for it originates and depends on it, so how could it oppose it? We mean by Sacred Law here the textual evidence duly transmitted and that which enjoys a consensus. As for questions on which scholars differ and which depend on weighing evidence and opinions, and on a scholar's capacity to think and aptitude, a saint may be given by inspiration the clear unambiguous truth, still in conformity to the legal principles and agreed-upon conditions, such as is not granted to those who derive rulings by exercising their intelligence and rational capacity.

Someone said, 'The Knowers and those who understand from God are also independent scholars (*mujtahid*), for they never transgress religion and the Sacred Law even for as little as the batting of an eyelid. However, those whose aptitude is deficient cannot understand what they have, nor their proofs, and so they oppose them and pronounce them ignorant and gone astray; for their sciences are beyond intelligence and rational thinking, which are veils that obstruct the said deficient people. We have already stated that the end-point for saints is the starting-point for Prophets and that no saint can ever reach the degree of the Prophets and their kind of revelation; they may only attain, by emulating them, to inspiration and unveiling.

A certain Knower said, '. . .'[01] He also said, 'The knowledge and understanding that people have of the Prophet ﷺ are [in proportion to all there is to know of him] like the moisture seeping out of the tied mouth of a waterskin [in proportion to all that the waterskin contains].'

The Difference between Revelation and Inspiration

There is a vast distance between the degree of sainthood and that of Prophecy, and also between the sciences of the Prophet that come from true revelation and the unveilings of the saints that come by inspiration. For the latter, although much higher than dream-visions, are many degrees below revelation, and there are many differences between them. Among them is, as mentioned above, that what comes by inspiration is never as clear as what comes by revelation. Also, there remains with it some hesitation. 'Alī alluded to that when he said, 'Were the cover [over Reality] to be removed, I would not increase in certainty.' And Abū al-Dardā' said, 'The believer

01 Missing word and garbled sentence.

looks from behind a thin veil. By God, it is the truth that He casts into their hearts and makes their tongues utter.'

Ghazālī says, 'Then this knowledge which is cast into the heart without prior planning, effort, striving, or reflection on the servant's part is divided into that which the servant knows not how or wherefrom it came; and that which is accompanied by awareness of the means by which it came, which is to see the angel who casts it into his heart. The first is called inspiration and insufflation into the heart, the second revelation. The latter is exclusive to the Prophets; the former includes saints and the élite; that which comes through rational deduction belongs to the scholars. The truth is that the heart is capable of receiving the truth of the reality of all things but is prevented from it by the five above reasons, for they are like a veil drawn between the mirror of the heart and the Guarded Tablet on which is inscribed all that God has decreed until Judgment Day. The way in which the reality of sciences is transmitted from the mirror of the Tablet to the mirror of the heart is like an image being projected from a mirror to another facing it. The veil between the two mirrors may sometimes be removed by hand, or by the wind when it blows. Similarly, the winds of gentle care may blow and remove the veil from the eye of the heart, so that it begins to reflect. . .[here ends the manuscript].

Prayer of the Drawn-Near

ḤABĪB AL-ḤASAN
IBN ṢĀLIḤ AL-BAḤR

Translator's Introduction

Ḥabīb al-Ḥasan ibn Ṣāliḥ ibn ʿAydarūs al Baḥr al-Jufrī al-ʿAlawī was born at al-Ḥawṭa, in the Ḥaḍramawt valley, in 1191/1777. He studied under a number of authoritative scholars and received the concentrated spiritual attention of the ʿAlawī masters of his day, becoming in his turn an authoritative scholar and spiritual master of the highest calibre.

Among Ḥabīb Ḥasan's treatises, the most precious from the Sufi point of view is one that reveals the inward secrets of the ritual prayer, giving a rare glimpse of what the real Knowers experience. It was produced at the request of the authoritative scholar and saint, Sayyid ʿAbd al-Raḥmān ibn Sulaymān al-Ahdal, the famous Grand *Muftī* of Zabīd in Northern Yemen[01]. It is the work of a realized man of God who writes entirely from personal experience, having reached the pinnacle of direct spiritual knowledge and thus being able to give a firsthand description of what such men as him experience each time they face the *Qibla* and raise their hands to signal their entry into the Divine Presence.

This treatise was originally printed in Cairo in 1383/1963 under the supervision of the late Shaykh Ḥasanayn Makhlūf, former Grand *Muftī* of Egypt, a man of immense erudition and sincerity and a confirmed lover of the ʿAlawīs, a great number of whose works he edited and published. He added to it a chapter of his own entitled 'The Prayer of the Humble,' intended to be more accessible to the ordinary reader. This chapter we have retained but shifted forward to precede the main treatise, since to be one of the Humble is a necessary preparation for moving further up the ladder and becoming one of the Drawn-Near.

Ḥabīb Ḥasan writes in a powerful and highly poetic style that does not

01 Sayyid ʿAbd al-Raḥmān ibn Sulaymān al-Ahdal was a famous North Yemeni scholar of Ḥusaynī descent who lived and taught at Zabīd. He died in 1248/1832.

lend itself easily to translation. Such concentrated treatises are so heavily laden with meanings that they need, and indeed often attract, voluminous commentaries. The intention here is not so much to clarify and explain every expression as to allow the reader a glimpse into what spiritual men such as the author, who was also an erudite scholar, receive in the way of Divine gifts.

The spiritual rank of the author was recognized by many great scholars and Knowers by God. It was confirmed by a man who was widely believed to be the greatest saint of his time, Sayyid Aḥmad ibn Idrīs[01]. Sayyid Aḥmad ibn ʿAlī al-Junayd recounted how in the course of one of their pilgrimages they had visited the great master as he was holding one of his teaching sessions. They found a large crowd in attendance, but were nevertheless allowed to read in the presence of the Shaykh. Sayyid Aḥmad al-Junayd read from the *Rashafāt*, the collection of Sufi poems by Ḥabīb ʿAbd al-Raḥmān Balfaqīh, detailing the progress of the seeker along the path. The Shaykh listened carefully, commenting on the poem by quoting for each of its verses a verse from the Qur'ān and a *Ḥadīth* of the Prophet ﷺ. Then Ḥabīb Ḥasan read his own '*Prayer of the Drawn-Near*'. The Shaykh said, 'If the author of this treatise is alive, he is worthy of being journeyed to on camelback[02].' One of his students said, 'Sayyidī, could he not simply be a describer?'—meaning that he was just reproducing a description heard from other sources. The Shaykh retorted sharply, 'Silence! Each vessel exudes what it contains[03].' Sayyid al-Junayd was about to say that the author was none other than the person who had just read the treatise, but Ḥabīb Ḥasan told him, 'Be quiet! Say nothing!'

Ḥabīb Ḥasan died in 1273/1857.

---

01 Sayyid Aḥmad ibn Idrīs was a famous Moroccan Sufi of Ḥasanī Idrisī descent. He studied in Morocco before emigrating to Makka, where he taught, held sessions of *dhikr*, and produced such illustrious disciples as al-Sanūsī, and al-Mirghanī, each of whom became the founder of a new *ṭarīqa*. He left Makka in 1234/1818–19 and met Sayyid ʿAbd al-Raḥmān ibn Sulaymān al-Ahdal in Zabīd during his trip to Yemen, before finally settling in Ṣabyā in ʿAsīr province, south of the Ḥijāz, where he died in 1253/1834.

02 An Arabic expression meaning that to meet the man in question would be well worth an arduous trip across deserts on camelback.

03 This line of poetry, which has long been a much-quoted proverb, signifies that a person's speech and behavior are reliable indications of what his heart contains.

Prayer of the Humble

BY SHAYKH ḤASANAYN MAKHLŪF

As you hear the Call to the Prayer, O Muslim, remember the terrifying call for the judgment on Resurrection Day, and hasten to respond![01]

As you purify your body, your clothes, and the place of your prayer, be careful also to purify your heart from sins and feel remorse for whatever you have neglected[02].

As you cover your outward shameful parts, do not omit to cover your inward shameful parts. Be remorseful for them, and fearful and ashamed before God ﷻ.

As you turn toward the *Qibla* to pray, turn away from all other than Him ﷻ, as you stand before Him, communing with Him.

As you stand upright, bow your head down and impose humility and abasement upon your heart.

Expel arrogance and pride from your heart and know that you are only a slave that He owns.

As you make your intention for the Prayer, intend resolutely to conform to His order for you to pray a complete prayer, avoiding whatever may nullify or ruin it.

---

01 The Shaykh starts by underlining the connection between this world and the Next, and the repercussions our actions have in the Hereafter.

02 In this and the next few lines the Shaykh links the outward to the inward elements of the Prayer, the inward here being the psychological but not yet the spiritual level, since he speaks of purity of intention, concentration, attentiveness, and qualities like humility and sincerity.

Be sincere with God ﷻ, in all this, hopeful for His recompense, fearful of His punishment, and wishing for His nearness.

Then impose upon yourself all that this treatise contains by way of description of the Prayer of the Drawn-Near[01].

Reverence, submission, poverty, abasement before God, and sincerity in acts of worship are all the fruits of faith, the results of certainty in His majesty Exalted is He, His immensity, and His might. These can only be perfected when the heart is present and the meanings of the recitations understood; when there is reverence for God, awe, hope and modesty. The first [presence of the heart] comes from belief in a Hereafter and in the insignificance of this world. The second [understanding the meanings of Scripture] comes from constant reflection and meditation. The third [reverence] comes from knowledge of the majesty of God and insignificance of the self. The fourth [awe] comes from knowledge of the omnipotence of God and His sovereignty. The fifth [hope] comes from knowledge of the kindness of God, His generosity and mercy. The sixth [shame] comes from knowledge of the defects of the self, its ailments, and lack of sincerity.

Al-Rabīʿ ibn Khaytham[02] used so much to lower his gaze and bow down his head, because of his extreme humility, that people thought him blind. When Ibn Masʿūd looked at him he used to say, '**And give glad tidings to the humble**'[117]. Once, as they walked together between blacksmiths' forges, [al-Rabīʿ] saw the bellows blowing and the fire ablaze; he fainted and remained unconscious for a whole day. As for ʿĀmir ibn ʿAbd Allāh[03], when he stood in prayer, they could beat drums and women could chatter as loudly as they wished, yet he heard nothing and remained unaware of them. Muslim ibn Yasār[04] was standing in prayer once when a pillar in the mosque collapsed; he felt nothing! Another virtuous man suffered from

---

01 This moves the worshiper to the third level. Having perfected the first, the outward or physical form of the Prayer, then the second, which is the psychological level, he must ascend to the third or spiritual level, which is the subject matter of the coming treatise.

02 Al-Rabīʿ ibn Khaytham, sometimes spelled Khuthaym (d. 67/686–7), was a Follower, a disciple of the great Companion ʿAbd Allāh ibn Masʿūd, and a transmitter of *Ḥadīth*s.

03 ʿĀmir ibn ʿAbd Allāh ibn al-Zubayr ibn al-ʿAwwām (d. 121/739) was a Follower known for his generosity, humility, and detachment from the world.

04 Muslim ibn Yasār was a Follower and transmitter of *ḥadīth*s. He died in 100/718–19.

gangrene of one of his extremities; they amputated it as he was praying, knowing that then he would feel nothing. A man was once asked, 'Do you recall any memories during your prayers?' He answered, 'Is there anything that I love more than the Prayer, that I should recall it?'

Be careful to maintain humility during your prayers as much as possible. Do your very best, and remember the greatness of Him whom you are addressing and your own insignificance. Try to imitate some of the things you know of the virtuous Predecessors in this matter, that God may grant you success in achieving the prayer of the Drawn-Near. Success is from God.

May God's blessings and peace be upon our Master Muḥammad, his Family, and his Companions.

Prayer of the Drawn-Near

BY ḤABĪB AL-ḤASAN IBN ṢĀLIḤ AL-BAḤR

In the Name of God, Most Merciful and Compassionate

All praise belongs to God, who has brought forth the 'secret of election'[01] from the fountainhead of existence[02], the beauty of which suffuses both the visible and invisible worlds[03].

May God's blessings and peace be upon our Master Muḥammad, the *Qibla* of the 'Spirits of the Throne'[04], the Solitary Being[05] in the Presence of the [Divine] Essence[06], the Mountain of the Manifestations of Benefaction[07],

---

01 It is stated in a *ḥadīth* that God created human beings in darkness, then cast His light upon them. Those who received this light were rightly-guided, and those who did not erred. [Tirmidhī, *Sunan*, 2642]

02 *'Ayn* (fountainhead) also means the 'eye', the 'thing in itself', or the 'essential nature' of a thing.

03 The 'visible worlds' include all that is perceptible to the ordinary human senses, while the invisible worlds include everything else, starting from the nearest subtle dimension and up to the highest Divine Station.

04 'The Spirits of the Throne' (*al-Arwāḥ al-'arshiyya*) may mean the archangels surrounding the Divine Throne, the spirits of the saints whose station is the Throne, or both.

05 The Solitary Being is he who was the first being to come into existence, the First Light, also called the Pen, the First Intellect, and the Muḥammadan Spirit, according to which of his aspects is envisaged.

06 The Divine Essence is the undifferentiated necessary being, before the deployment of the Names and Attributes that precedes the appearance of creation.

07 'Mountains' in the expressions of the Sufis always denotes the station of Moses 🕊. The Mountain is thus the locus where Divine Attributes manifest, this being the heart of the Knower by God.

the Point of Action[01] from which are deployed the centers of the *Ṣamadiyya* Lights[02]; and upon his Family and Companions, who are the rays of his light, the stars [surrounding] his full moon, and the interpreters of both his prohibitions and his commands.

To proceed: As the Prayer is the spirit of all good works, the reality of the degrees of connection[03] and union[04], the subtle secret of existence in pre-eternity[05], the thing by which appears the Lordly light hidden within the moulds of forms[06], it is the duty of him whose insight has been illuminated by God and whose inward He has purified to concentrate on it with recollection, traversing the obstacles along its ladder, that he may drink of its fresh pure beverage[07].

Should he then cleanse himself of turbidity and liberate himself from the

---

01 The Point is the First Determination, which when acted upon by the Essence produces level after level of existence. It is the aforementioned Solitary Being, First Light, or First Intellect.

02 *Ṣamadiyya* is derived from the Divine Name *al-Ṣamad*, He who is the Self-Sufficient Lord and to whom everyone turns for their needs, which only He is able to fulfill. It is one of the Names of the Divine Essence and the lights here mentioned are its reflections in the mirror of creation by first being reflected in the Solitary Being. The First Light then divides into other lights, these being the lights of the Prophets and the saints, which then radiate to reach the rest of humanity. The *Ṣamadiyya* Lights are thus the lights which are the primary radiation and reflection of the First Light, starting from the other Prophets and the Family and Companions of our Prophet ﷺ, then subsequent saints till the Last Day.

03 Connection (*Waṣl*): The seeker strives along the Path until he reaches the doorstep, at which point he is connected to the higher worlds. Then he arrives at the nearness and acceptance that lead to contemplation. Just as the Prophet ﷺ is the mountain from which the saints receive the outpouring of Divine mercies and bounties, so are the saints the secondary centers from which the rest of the Muslims receive theirs.

04 Union (*ittiṣāl*) means the absorption of the relative in the contemplation of the Absolute, never the joining of two separate entities.

05 There are a number of Arabic expressions the only English equivalent of which are the terms "eternity" and "eternal". *Al-Azal* is eternity preceding this point in time. *Al-Abad* is eternity from this point onward. *Al-Qadīm* is Existence without beginning. *Al-Sarmadī* is the existent without end.

06 Creation is the manifestation of combinations of Divine Attributes as reflected in forms and events.

07 Spiritual beverage consists of the lights of the higher worlds descending into the heart that is concentrated in prayer. It is the *wārid* that the author mentions further ahead in the treatise; see p. 81, footnote.

bonds of [attending to] others[01], he will stand in pure humility and broken-heartedness, submissive before the power of Majesty and attentive to the Beauty of the Beloved. He will then fervently ask and implore to be granted firmness when he comes to stand before the Immense, the Most High.

Then he says *Allāhu Akbar* (God is Greater)[02], realizing that only God is great in his heart, casting aside everything that is not Him, seeking His satisfaction. For He is the Lord and Patron of all things, from Him they originate, and to Him is their end. Let him beware of his deeds giving the lie to his words, should there remain in his mind anything to be sought or loved other than God. When he is with the Immense, the Omnipotent, he should not be contented with the insignificant and small. Let him cast away all his worries and witness how He sustains every known thing[03].

Then he confirms with his tongue what is in his heart by saying: '*Wajjahtu wajhiya* (I have turned my face) meaning the face of my heart [which is my attention] and my entire resolution, with abasement, to Him ﷻ, for He is the Formidable; with hope in Him, for He is the Forbearing, the Compassionate; and with reliance on Him, for He is the Powerful, the Omnipotent.[04] *Li-lladhī faṭara s-samāwāti wa l-arḍ* (toward the One who created the heavens and the earth).' At this point the darkness will depart from him and, witnessing the fountainhead of liberality and generosity, he will no longer harbor any wish, whether earthly or heavenly, since both

---

01 'Others', *al-aghyār*, is a term literally denoting everything other than God, but frequently used for everything either not pointing directly to Him, or cutting one off from Him. Divine Prophets, Scriptures, and saints are direct signs of him and are therefore not considered *aghyār*.

02 *Allāh Akbar*: God is greater, greater than all creation put together, greater than anything conceived or imagined, greater than to be associated in one's thoughts with anything else, greater than to be known by His creation.

03 The contemplation of the Name '*al-Qayyūm*', the Sustainer, who provides all things with existence and provisions at each instant. Should His sustaining of creation be withdrawn, it would instantaneously vanish by simply ceasing to exist.

04 Ḥabīb Ḥasan means that the face we turn is that of our metaphorical relationship with God. We can understand that it is metaphorical because in the eyes of the Knowers by God we do not, in Reality, exist—only God does—and there can be no relationship between that which exists and that which does not. He then goes on to say that the reason why the creation of the heavens and the earth was specifically mentioned is that they are the greatest creations witnessed by the eyes of man and were created for his sake.

heaven and earth and all that they contain exist by His generosity and are sustained by His attributes.

Ḥanīfan (upright and straight), turning neither to the right by placing one's hopes in other than Him, nor to the left by fearing other than Him.[01]

Musliman (a Muslim), with submission and docility, wanting nothing but what He wants, never relying or depending on other than Him, for there is no other[02].

Wa mā anā min al-mushrikīn (and I am not of those who associate) my own wishes with His, or waver in my love of Him. How could I prefer to Him another beloved, since none can exist save by His grace? How could I desire, concomitantly with desiring Him, something that can be sustained only by Him?[03]

Inna ṣalātī (My prayer) in His presence is a gift to me from His mercy; the same mercy that has brought submission, surrender, favor, and grace.

Wa nusukī (and my rituals): the existence of my obedience to Him, submission to His command, patient endurance of His decrees, and ardor in thanking Him.

Wa maḥyāya (and my life), which is to be attached to His Attributes and to witness His gracious favors and kindness.[04]

Wa mamātī (and my death): my absence from my own existence in His

---

01 *Ḥanīfan*: This is a term used to denote the Abrahamic religion prior to Islam, as well as the rectitude and uprightness resembling the *fiṭra* as renewed by Islam. Ḥabīb Hasan explains that by the aforementioned turning of the face, one veers away from giving any attention to other than God, whether this other be sensible or intelligible.

02 Islam is complete submission, so that the Muslim is he who is entirely compliant with God's orders and prohibitions, and surrendered to His will. According to the author, this is nothing but being a *Ḥanīf*, a follower of Abraham ﷺ, who, **When his Lord said to him, 'Surrender!' said, 'I surrender to the Lord of all beings'**. [Qur'ān, 2:131] Then he surrendered by offering his possessions to his guests, his son to the sacrifice, and his own heart and his wife to God by leaving her without any source of food or water in Makka, at the command of his Lord.

03 We notice how here, as in the rest of the treatise, the author altogether ignores the immediate outward meaning and confines himself to the inward dimensions of *Tawḥīd*. *Shirk* is to associate another deity with God, be it an idol, a phenomenon of nature, a human being, or a mythological personage. Sufis, however, acutely aware of what the term 'Absolute' implies, concentrate on inward *Tawḥīd*, that of the heart.

04 To be alive is to be aware of God and the action of His Attributes in creation at all times, and thus of the constant flow of graces to which a creature is subject; to be dead is to be lost in the ocean of unawareness teeming with confusing secondary

contemplation[01], and my absence from my contemplation of Him in the subsistence of His existence[02].

Li-Llāhi (are for God), meaning that He is the One who stood me in these [actions] and favored me with them, with neither ability nor power on my part, as it is He, *Rabbi l-ʿālamīn* (Lord of all Beings) who draws [some] nearer and drives [others] away, makes some wretched and others happy. Everyone submits to His coercion and is in awe of His glory. He humbles whomsoever He wishes and He exalts whomsoever He wishes. None can alter His decisions as concerns what He does or undoes; none assists Him in creating what He brings into existence, and none assists Him in destroying it.[03]

Lā sharīka lahu (He has no associates) who resemble Him in His Lordship; for even those the highest beings, those who are the spirit of the universe, are His creation, His slaves, and He disposes of them by His domination and directs them with His knowledge.

---

causes, phenomena that when seen as independently effective phenomena cut one off from God.

01 The death that we know is that of the body. Another death, as mentioned above, is to be dead because inattentive to God and attentive to creation. The real death, however, is that of the soul, which means its death or absence from all other than God and presence solely with Him. This is the slave's extinction in the Lordly Presence (*fanā*'). The author once explained the concept of *fanā*' by saying that first, there is extinction to creation, then to one's own soul, then to one's will. Then comes extinction in Divine actions, which means that one's blameworthy actions are changed into praiseworthy ones. Next comes extinction in the Attributes, which means that one's bad attributes are changed into good ones. Finally, there is extinction in the Essence, which is to become extinct to one's own contemplation, and this is only for the *Ṣiddīqūn*. This comes in flashes and does not last; were it to do so, the human attributes would perish. In this condition one is unaware of one's sensory perception, absent to them as it were.

02 The next stage is the slave's return to creation (*baqā*'), subsisting by his Lord, veiled neither from his Lord by creation, nor by the Lordly lights from creation.

03 Ḥabīb Ḥasan remarks that this formula is based on the following passages from the Qur'ān: **I have turned my face toward the One who created the heavens and the earth, upright and straight, and I am not of those who associate.** [2:135] Say, 'My prayer, and my rituals, and my life, and my death are for God, the Lord of all beings.' [6:162] According to him, God commands the Muslims to emulate Abraham 🖎, in all he said or did, for He says in the Qur'ān, **So follow the religion of Abraham, who was upright and straight and was not of those who associate.** [3:95]

Wa bi-dhālika umirtu (thus am I commanded to do): and for this I was created.

Wa anā mina l-muslimīn (and I am one of the Muslims), who are truly aware of His domination and subjugation of everything, have surrendered to the sovereignty of His glory, cling to the curtains of His mercy[01], and halt at their inability to comprehend the reality of the knowledge of Him.

You should then seek His protection from the subterfuges of the 'Chief Deceiver', and invoke the protection of God's might against his cunning and temptations by saying:

Aʿūdhu bi-llāhi mina sh-Shayṭāni r-rajīm (I seek the protection of God against the repudiate Devil): also intend to seek protection from all 'others', but mainly from the thoughts of the soul and the appetites of the body.

Say *Bismillāh* (In the Name of God) with the realization that everything stands by His Name and is surrounded by His knowledge. Realize that divinity penetrates all of existence and manifest through its wisdom in every limit that is set and every being that is limited, as in every being that is drawn near or banished away.

When you say *Ir-Raḥmāni r-Raḥīm* (The Most Merciful and Compassionate)[02], witness His mercy embracing all existence. He is *Raḥmān*, Most Merciful, by bringing created beings into existence, and *Raḥīm*, Compassionate, by sustaining [those He has thus created].

Accordingly, give Him, who is the All-Praiseworthy, His due of praises by saying, *Al-ḥamdu li-llāhi* (All praise and thanks belong to God), for His praises exhaust all praise, in sum and in detail.

Bring to your awareness that you are the deputy of all existence[03] [chosen] to face this generosity, for He has made you the mediator in bringing

---

01 This situation is likened to the desperate clinging to the curtains and door of the Kaʿba door by pilgrims determined to let their Lord hear their pleas.

02 *Al-Raḥmān* is the Infinitely Merciful in His Essence, through whose mercy creation comes into being in the first place and then envelops every creature at every instant so that its existence is sustained. *Al-Raḥīm* is the Merciful in His dealings with creation, and is also the selectively Merciful, who provides for His creatures, makes them compassionate to each other, guides whomsoever He will to the Straight Path, aids them in their good works, rewards them for them, and so leads them to the Garden.

03 Mankind as *Khalīfa*, or vicegerent, is also creation's deputy before the Creator. Mankind's representative, the true *Khalīfa*, is the Perfect Man, whose awareness extends from the lowest to the highest degrees of existence—not ordinary veiled

forth every existent thing and in sustaining everything that is sustained; for you are the secret of existence[01]. Know therefore the worth of your own creation and the magnitude of your Creator. As for bringing forth, it is from His ﷻ saying, '**God It is who created seven heavens, and of earth their like. Between them the Command descends, that you may know that God is powerful over everything and that God encompasses everything in knowledge**[118].'

And as for sustaining, it is part of the meaning of His ﷻ saying, '**And He has subjected to you what is in the heavens and what is in the earth, all together, from Him.**'[119]

For the sustaining of existence is by the dawning upon it of His ﷻ light, and dense bodies cannot bear His light unless they have already received the 'light of electhood', as can be witnessed by him the mirror of whose heart has been illuminated. From the visible [manifestation of light] pours down from the clouds physical rain, while from its invisible [manifestation], the fountains of secrets overflow with hidden lights.

You should then stand under the sway of glory and majesty, descend to the low 'place of descent'[02] and witness '**Whatever blessing you have, it comes from God.**'[120]

Say *Rabbi l-ʿālamīn* (Lord of the Worlds), then witness how the worlds stand under compulsion, docilely led to what has been decreed, unable either to attract good to themselves or repel evil. At this point you will come upon the pleasure of abasement and insignificance[03], and fall back upon the mercy of the Generous, the Forgiving, the Forbearing, the Shielding; fall back with courteous neediness and poverty, saying *ar-Raḥmāni* (the

---

man, whose awareness is restricted to infinitesimal portions of the physical and subtle domains.

01 Since the universe was created for mankind and man, being the only creature able to fully know its Lord, was created for God, it can be said that man is the secret of the universe. However, man remains only potentially the secret of existence, to become so in actuality only when the degree of Knower by God is reached.

02 This refers to the material dimension, the level at which commands issuing from the Divine Presence and descending through the multiple levels of existence come to rest.

03 It is only when the lowest point of self-abasement and insignificance is reached that God allows access to the experience of His absolute transcendence and significance, which is the ultimate pleasure. Complete poverty in the slave attracts the Divine filling of the void with His light.

Most Merciful) who has caused you to qualify to stand before Him and made you to address Him and commune with Him by saying, *r-Raḥīm* (the Compassionate), who has compassion for you despite your weakness, shortcomings, wrongdoing, and untruthfulness. His mercy for you preceded your being created and given form.

Then negate your confusion and delusion, witness the descent of special mercy on your mountain[01] and the 'robe of guardianship' on your form, lose in His special sovereignty your awareness by saying *Māliki yawmi d-dīn* (Sovereign of the Day of Judgment) when the eye of certainty becomes unveiled and manifest truth becomes clear.

When you come to from the state of bedazzlement induced by Majesty, rise in powerlessness and gratitude, and witness His doing everything for you in the state of Beauty. Say *Iyyāka naʿbudu* (You it is that we worship) out of Your generosity, grace, kindness and favor, *Wa iyyāka nastaʿīn* (and Your help it is that we request) in reliance on You and certainty, implicitly and explicitly. Then your fear will abate and your hope will expand, so ask Him by Him for the perfection of rectitude, by saying *Ihdina ṣ-ṣirāṭa l-mustaqīm* (Guide us to the Straight Path). Intend by that the source from which the Prophet ﷺ drinks, which is the 'fountain of life', by which I mean the spirit of the *Sharīʿa*, the body of which is the perfection of rectitude. *Ṣirāṭa lladhīna anʿamta ʿalayhim* (the path of those whom You have favored) with the delight of Your Speech and the beauty of Your kindness and approach. These are the Prophets and the *Ṣiddīqūn* whom You have chosen for obedience to You, favored with Your presence, delighted with Your contemplation, and introduced to Your proximity in Your abode of honour.

Ghayri l-maghḍūbi ʿalayhim (not those upon whom is Your wrath), which deprives them of obedience to You and from following Your Path, thereby establishing Your argument [against them]. *Wa la ḍ-ḍāllīn* (nor those who are astray), whom You have veiled, deprived of hearing the delightful address, and barred from intoxication with the nectar beverage.

Humble before His august presence, standing at His door, certain of a response from Him, say *Āmīn!*

Then recite a *sūra* and witness Him in His Words. Know that it is only

01 The reference is again to the mountain of Moses ﷺ, which is the locus of Divine manifestations. This is the human spirit. As for the body, it receives the 'mantle of protection' that prevents it from doing wrong and keeps it on the Straight Path.

by Him that you utter those words. Judge yourself and confess to your neglect in conforming to His orders and prohibitions, increase your desire for what He promised and made you hope for. At this point you will find in every verse, nay in every word, nay in every letter, a captivating meaning, a subtle secret, and a lofty state.[01]

Then bow down, in submission to Him and shyness, since He has made you one of those [admitted] into His Presence. [Bow down] in reverence for the majesty of His might and the loftiness of His glory. Realize that everything bows down to Him in awe, in submission to His might and docility before His power[02].

Say *Subḥāna Rabbiya l-ʿAẓīmi wa bi-ḥamdih* (Transcendent is my Formidable Lord and [praised] by His praises [to Himself]). Make your *tasbīḥ* an attribution of transcendence to Him and shyness of Him, since you are addressing Him despite His majesty and eminence, and your abasement and weakness, your lowliness and His loftiness. Then fill your heart with delight with Him and joy at His proximity, for He has attributed your servitude to Him[03] and made you worthy to stand before Him. Make adequate therefore your praises of Him and remember His graces, gifts, nearness and assistance.

Then straighten up, in delight at His nearness and pride in His love, and say *Samiʿa llāhu li-man ḥamidah* (God hears him who praises Him). He hears him, that is, with acceptance, responsiveness, satisfaction and love, for otherwise He hears everything and is nearer to things heard than that which hears [meaning the ear]—indeed, He is nearer to the thing heard than itself. This is where expression fails, indications are silenced, and the secret of the Beloved appears.

Then say *Rabbanā* (Our Lord), intending with the pronoun 'Our' all beings in general, and those possessed of knowledge in particular.

Laka l-ḥamdu (Praise belongs to You), a praise that exhausts all merits,

---

01 This is what the Knowers by God have always asserted, from the days of the Companions onward: that each of the Qur'ān's components possesses dimensions of meaning of its own, so that *sūra*s, passages, verses, individual words or letters, all have meanings that God reveals to whichever of His devoted servants He chooses.

02 The act of bowing down, or *rukūʿ*, from which comes from the same triliteral root as the term *rakʿa* (cycle of ritual prayer), is here perceived as a response to manifestations of Majesty.

03 By calling you ʿAbd Allāh, Slave of God—an honor beyond which no honor exists.

and is adequate to the favors received and equal to the surplus[01]. Witness that any praise for other than Him is figurative, whereas for Him it is real; for all praise ultimately returns to Him, while also originating in Him from His generosity. Feel in your heart the following: 'None is capable of praising You but You, of thanking You, but You! I therefore praise You with that with which You have praised Yourself.' However, He has attributed the praising to you and was content to receive it from you. Bring to mind, therefore, the following address: 'Praise belongs to You as You have praised Yourself and as befits the majesty of Your Countenance and the immensity of Your sovereignty, from each one of Your creation, numbering as many as the atoms of the world, multiplied by the number of breaths and instants, stillnesses and intentions, thoughts and utterances, good deeds and bad ones, and all letters, to subsist as long as You do, with no end to its eternity, no annihilation to its perpetuity, and no limit to its permanence.'

Say *Mil'a s-samāwāti wa mil'a l-arḍi wa mil'a mā shi'ta min shay'in ba'd* (sufficient to fill the heavens and the earth and whatever You may wish beyond that), intending that each of these praises be as mentioned above, and intending by 'beyond that' the Throne, the Pedestal, and all beings, then the open space of *Tawḥīd*, which is limitless[02].

Then say *Ahlu th-thanā'i* (Worthy to be lauded), meaning 'You are the One who lauds Himself, for none can laud You save by Your help, favor, grace and mercy,' *Wa l-majd* (and glorified) for none possess glory other than You. Every glory is from Your glory, every being deserving of praise is Your creation, Your servant. *Aḥaqqu mā qāla l-'abdu* (the truest thing a servant has said) in the perfection of his servitude and the obliteration of his human attributes, the annihilation of his claims and his awareness of his acts, when the light of his electhood dawns upon him. *Wa kullunā laka 'ābīd* (and we are all Your servants), for You have disposal of our outward and inward being.' Now realize His Lordship over you in all your movements and standstills, attribute to yourself all blameworthy attributes, while witnessing in your Lord all noble Attributes.

Say *Lā māni'a limā a'ṭayta* (None can withhold what You bestow), for

---

01 God says in the Qur'ān, [14:7] '**If you are thankful I shall certainly increase you.**' This means: 'If you thank Me for every favor you receive, I shall increase my favors upon you accordingly.'

02 *Tawḥīd* is unification. When all things come together in the One, constraints and limits disappear and one enters the open space that is infinity.

power is impossible for any other than You, since there is no existence but Yours[01], and no witnessing save by Your light.

Wa lā muʿṭiya limā manaʿṭa (and none can bestow what You withhold), for You alone decide whom to withhold from and banish, and You alone know whom to make fortunate and whom to make wretched.

Wa lā yanfaʿu dha l-jaddi minka l-jadd (The wealth of the wealthy avails him nothing with You), for created beings cannot benefit from one another, since all benefit is from and by You.

Then prostrate yourself before Him, for in your standing upright was the witnessing of His sustaining you and nearness from you, since you were upright by His Attribute, so that by Him you now become absent to yourself. This is the station of Extinction (*Fanā'*). Then the flash of Subsistence (*Baqā'*) appears, by your witnessing your remoteness from Him, simultaneously with His nearness to you. You then witness His loftiness and greatness, and His nearness and mercy, so you prostrate yourself. For the meaning of prostration is to abase yourself as if you were dead, denuded of the attributes of life, and therefore denuded of the attributes of your soul. The meaning of drawing near in His ﷻ Words, '**Prostrate yourself and draw near**'[121] will appear to you, so that you say *Subḥāna Rabbiya l-Aʿlā wa bi-ḥamdih* (Transcendent is my Lord Most High, and [praised] by His praises); you negate His being near to you, but cling to His Attribute which manifests in you. At this point you will be lost in the open space of Unity (*Tawḥīd*).

At this point the people of this description, may God be pleased with them, vary in their states. For some the *wārid*[02] is direct knowledge, for others it is love, and for others still awe.

He whose *wārid* is direct knowledge, his heart roams the worlds of the *Mulk* and *Malakūt*, and the hidden secrets and radiant states are unveiled to him.

He whose *wārid* is love, unveiled for him are intimacy and welcome, as well as drawing near to the Beloved.

---

01 There is nothing that exists by itself save the Absolute; there is none who can give or withhold but He Who has.

02 The *wārid* is literally 'that which arrives'. See p.81, footnote. In this context, it refers to the various spiritual states, including inspiration, which descend from the higher worlds on the heart of the servant.

He whose *wārid* is awe, the *Jabarūt* is unveiled for him and he prostrates himself upon the *Bahamūt*[01].

He who is a center for the Attributes, and upon whose heart the lights of the Essence flash, becomes extinct in the Essence and subsistent by the Attributes. He flees from the awesome Attributes to the Attributes of boundless compassion, and says, *Aʿūdhu bi-riḍāka min sakhaṭik* (I take protection in Your satisfaction from Your wrath). When he sees the Attributes of rigor and coercion, he flees to those of forbearance and forgiveness, and says, *Wa aʿūdhu bi-muʿāfātika min ʿuqūbatik* (And I take protection in the wellbeing You grant from the chastisement You mete out).

And whenever the light of the Essence shines in his heart, he becomes able to express the Names and Attributes, ascend the highest degrees, and say, *Wa aʿūdhu bika mink* (And I seek Your protection from You!). For no other being remains in existence besides Him, nor does any other remain to be seen but Him. Existence is sentenced to annihilation and depletion, a witness to negation, and all that remains is the self-subsistence of the Necessarily Existent.

At this point signs become ineffective and words silenced, and he returns with powerlessness and brokenheartedness, abasement and poverty, to cast himself on the carpet of humility and neediness. He will know his own lowly attributes and cling to the majestic attributes of his Master. He will then sit up saying *Rabbī* (my Lord), as he witnesses His taking care of him and managing his affairs at every moment, and His compassion for him even before his form was created.

Ighfir lī (forgive me) what You know of my errors and sins,
wa rḥamnī (and have mercy on me) in my neediness and brokenheartedness,
wa jburnī (and mend me) in my weakness and abasement,
wa rfaʿnī (and raise me) from the depths of my states to the height of the presence of Your overflowing secret,
wa rzuqnī (and provide for me) in my times of difficulty and scarcity,
wa hdinī (and guide me) away from my error and perplexity,
wa ʿāfinī (and grant me safety) from my own planning and choices.

---

01 *Bahamūt*: this term denotes the lowest level of universal existence, the bestial, so the worshiper, facing the manifestation of Divine Majesty, prostrates by placing his forehead upon the lowest level that a created being can reach: total abasement in the face of Infinite Majesty.

You should then do the same in the second prostration and all other *rakʿas*.

After prostrating, sit in *iftirāsh*[01] for the first *tashahhud*, aware that you are before your Master. Assume a light sitting posture in reverence for Him in whose Presence you are, not prolonging it, for *iftirāsh* is the attribute of one who is subdued, sitting with courtesy, soon to rise.

Feel your sitting before Him, and that He is nearer to you than the nearest thing. Fill your heart with reverence and modesty of Him, and say, *At-taḥiyyāt* (Greetings). Remember that everything greets Him for the abundance of His gifts, asking for His mercy and good pleasure. When you say *ul-mubārakāt* (that are blessed) witness Him as both the greeter and the greeted. When you say *uṣ-ṣalawāt* (and prayers) remember the greeting of the people of nearness and the address of the people of love, and say, *uṭ-ṭayyibātu* (that are the best), pure, unblemished by the darkness of the self, moving in the assemblies of holiness, inhabited by the lights of intimacy, for in them none other than Him exists, *li-Llāh* (to God). You are then extinct to all others, drowned in the oceans of light, until when the eye of your inner sight is painted with the Light of Lights, the Secret of Secrets, the Chosen Prophet, you will say, *As-salāmu ʿalayka ayyuha n-Nabiyyu* (Peace be upon you, O Prophet). You will know how God protected him from all imperfections and defects, a protection the like of which no ancient or contemporary man ever received. *Wa raḥmatu llāhi wa barakātuh* (and the mercy and blessings of God): that is, His mercy that is specific to the Prophet and His blessings that overflow upon him, before overflowing upon the holy assemblies, and from them upon all the worlds, visible and invisible. Then say, *As-salāmu ʿalaynā wa ʿalā ʿibādi llāhi ṣ-ṣāliḥīn* (Peace be upon us and all virtuous servants of God) which is pardon and forgiveness, mercy and satisfaction, good news and security. Witness the assemblies of Prophets and saints and their drawing sustenance from his ﷺ presence.

Then turn your sight away from others to contemplate the King, the All-Compeller, and say *Ashhadu an lā ilāha illa Llāh* (I testify that there is no other god than God). At this point you will see none in His Presence, Exalted is He, but the Chosen One ﷺ. Then you say, *Wa ashhadu anna Muḥammadan Rasūlu llāh* (and I testify that Muḥammad is the Messenger of God).

---

01 *Iftirāsh* means to sit on one's left foot turned on its side underneath one's thigh and keep the right foot upright, toes on the ground and heel up.

Then remember that he is the mediator in attaining to this Presence, and ask the Generous, the Formidable, in whose Presence you are, to reward him, by saying *Allāhumma ṣalli ʿalā Muḥammad* (O God, bless Muḥammad).

Then stand up and repeat what we have just described.

When you reach the last *tashahhud* (the two testifications just described), remember in your heart that you are now permitted to sit, so sit with pleasure, and ask Him for your wishes and desires, which He causes you to desire, and ask for His protection from your fears of what He has warned you about. Acknowledge your powerlessness and incapacity to gain any of your wishes or escape [any of your fears] save by Him. At this point you will find great delight in His noble address and gentle reproaches; you will feel estrangement at having to leave this immense favor, which you will never leave without having received generous treatment.

O God make us of those whom You have favored, chosen, drawn near, and pulled closer, so that You delight us in the assemblies of Your proximity and intoxicate us with the nectar of Your love! Make not our share mere wandering and idle chatter. You are the Generous, the Bestower! Cover our defects with forgiveness and take over all our affairs with kindness and graciousness. Make our final end the Abode of Honor and Good Pleasure, O You who show mercy to the neglectful, support those who stumble, and accept repentance from the repentant!

May God's blessings and peace be upon our Master Muḥammad, his Family, and his Companions. All Praise belongs to God, Lord of the Worlds.

This blessed treatise is concluded. It is entitled *Bestowing the Gift of the 'Prayer of the Drawn-Near' upon the Elect among Believers and Perpetuating the Pleasure and Delight of Nearness to the Lord of the Worlds.'* It is also called *'Intimate Communion of the Lover with the Beloved with that which is the Intention and Goal.'*

All praise belongs to God, Lord of the Worlds. May God's blessings and peace be upon our Master Muḥammad, his Family, and his Companions.

The Seven Stages of a Human Being

BY ḤABĪB AḤMAD
IBN ZAYN AL-ḤABASHĪ

Translator's Introduction

The following short treatise by Ḥabīb Aḥmad ibn Zayn al-Ḥabashī is an example of how, along with solid foundations in *Sharīʿa*, ʿAlawī knowledge possesses the full depth of spiritual insight. Most of the monumental writings of Ḥabīb Aḥmad ibn Zayn resemble Imām al-Ḥaddād's in that they go beyond the purely outward to open a path toward the inward, but stop short of delving too deeply into spiritual realities so as not to cause confusion among students. The exceptions are the few short works where Ḥabīb Aḥmad briefly comments on certain poems of Imām al-Ḥaddād at the latter's bidding; and there too, as in the present treatise, it is noticeable that he confines himself to subtle allusions rather than a full commentary.

The subject of this treatise is rather unusual, for it deals with the correspondence between the seven stages the human foetus passes through, as outlined in the Qur'ān, and the stages of the spiritual Path. What embryology has to do with Sufism seems at first sight difficult to fathom. However, those aware of the correspondences between the various dimensions of Reality will comprehend how it can be just one more example of the ways in which the imprint of Divine Unicity pervades the universe, so that there is always a correspondence between one order of reality and another—outwardly and inwardly, cosmically, physically, mentally and spiritually.

In the Name of God, Most Merciful
and Compassionate, and it is His help that we seek

All praise be to God be praised, and may His blessings and peace be upon our master Muḥammad, his Family, and his Companions.

The following *ḥadīth* is quoted by scholars of jurisprudence, may God have mercy on them, and they have discussed it at length and interpreted it in widely divergent manners: *The manner of purification of your vessels, should they be licked by a dog, is to wash them seven times, one of these with dust*[01]. This *ḥadīth* contains an allusion to the seven stages of a human being[02]. God ﷻ says, **He has created you in stages**[122]. The first stage is that of the **extract of clay**, the second that of the **droplet in a secure receptacle**, the third that of the **clinging clot**, the fourth that of the **morsel of flesh**, the fifth that of the **bare bones**, the sixth that of the **covered bones**, and the seventh that of the **different creature**, which is the human being who is subject to Providence.

He ﷻ says, **And We have created man from an extract of clay, then We set him, a droplet in a secure receptacle, then We created of the droplet a clinging clot, then We created of that clot a morsel of flesh, then We created of that lump bones, then We produced him as a different creature. So blessed is God, the fairest of creators!**[123]

The above-mentioned **different creature** is equivalent to **the best constitution**[03], which is the original nature (*fiṭra*) of every newborn[04]. **Then We**

---

01 Nasā'ī, *al-Sunan al-Kubrā*, 69; Muslim, *Ṣaḥīḥ*, 422; Abū Dāwūd, *Sunan*, 66; Ibn Mājah, *Sunan*, 359.

02 Here the author leaves the level of jurisprudence behind and moves to the level of allusive inferences, whereby multiple dimensions of meaning are understood from a single sentence.

03 **We indeed created man in the best constitution, then reduced him to the lowest of the low.** Qur'ān, 95:4, 5.

04 A *ḥadīth* states: *At birth, the nature of every newborn is the original human one* (fiṭra),

reduced him to the lowest of the low[124], which is when he concentrates so much on the outward forms and is so preoccupied with his lowly bestial appetites and perceptions that he forgets the lofty world of the spirit, the quality of which is intelligible proximity[01] to the Divine Presence. For the origin of all human souls is one, the differences arising from contiguity with dark, physical bodies. One person's superiority over another is proportionate to how well each one's temperament is balanced and possessed of inner harmony. The better the balance and the more even the temperament, the greater the soul's attraction to its spiritual world, its travelling to its holy homeland, and its illumination by the Pen with which God 'teaches man what he knows not[02]' and inscribes within the hearts of saints faith and wisdom. This is none other than the First Intellect and the Spirit, with which believers are strengthened, which is the Light of our Prophet Muḥammad ﷺ, his origin. God ﷻ says, **And it is God who brought you forth from your mothers' wombs knowing nothing, and who has appointed for you hearing and sight and hearts, that you may be thankful**[125]. Thankfulness is to use all the appointed favors in that for which they were created, namely the devotional activities that draw one nearer to God ﷻ, through faith in Him and His Messenger, conformity, obedience, and the fulfillment of those Divine injunctions received through His Messenger. These deliver one from the snares of one's formal nature and physical appetites. The latter lead to that which is alluded to in the Divine Verses where He ﷻ says, **Thus did Our signs come to you, but you forgot them**[126]; **And We made a pact with Adam before, but he forgot**[127]. For he who pursues only the requirements of the body is but **walking prone upon his face**[128], so he is blind in this life and will be blind in the Next. When he comes to ask **Why have You raised me blind, when I used to see**[129]? for I was in the **best constitution**[130], God will reply, **Thus did Our signs come to you, but you forgot them**[131].

When the servant believes, accepts, and then makes of his body a mount to be ridden in his approach to the Presence, he will have deserved to be

---

and then his parents turn him into a Jew, a Christian, or a Zoroastrian.' (Bukhārī, *Ṣaḥīḥ*, 1358, 4775)

01 The author is concerned to emphasize that the proximity in question is of an intelligible, not a spatial nature, since the Absolute cannot be 'located' somewhere where He can be approached.

02 A reference to Qur'ān, 96:4-5: **Who teaches by the Pen; teaches man that which he knows not.**

told, **except those who believe and do good works**[01]; for his efforts to draw nigh and his following the Straight Path shall elevate him.

The **different creature**, which is the degree of humanity, has seven levels, corresponding to the seven levels and stages of the body. That which corresponds to the **extract from mud** is the descent of the spirit, which is its directing its attention to the body so as to manage its affairs, to act upon it without dwelling in it or physically occupying it; nor does [the spirit's] acting on it extend beyond it, or (. . .)[02] This is the first stage of the **different creature**.

The second stage, corresponding to the **droplet**, is one's beginning to acquire the ability to discern, understand injunctions, engage in acts of worship, and refrain from forbidden things.

The third stage, corresponding to the **clinging clot**, is to strive in the above-mentioned endeavors and work in earnest to balance one's temperament and achieve harmony.

The fourth stage, corresponding to the **morsel**, is to achieve purity from blemishes, concentrating on enlightenment, and distancing oneself from one's bodily nature and its filth.

The fifth stage, corresponding to the **bare bones**, is to understand Realities, reflect on them, and deduce them.

The sixth stage, corresponding to **covering the bones with flesh**, is to be invigorated with essential realities and realize the higher entities in their true manner and mode.

The seventh stage, corresponding to the **different creature**, is to concentrate entirely on God, Transcendent and Exalted is He, losing oneself in Him so as to forget all others, and acquire the reality of **Say: 'God!'**[03] With this the human vessel is purified completely from the impurity of the tongue of the demonic dog of lusts, having been washed seven times, the first being with mud, which is dust mixed with water.

The human being is the **different creature.** The sign of one's having become human[04] is the presence of inclination toward intellectual compre-

01 **[I swear] by the Afternoon! Man is indeed in the way of loss, save those who believe and do good works, and enjoin upon each other the truth, and enjoin upon each other patient endurance.** Qur'ān, 95:6.

02 There is a word missing from the text.

03 **Say: 'God!', then leave them to play at their prattle.** Qur'ān, 6:91.

04 'Human' here is equivalent to 'Adamic'; and since Adam was a Prophet, to be Adamic

hension, taking pleasure in spiritual matters, and moving away from physical pleasures, since the latter will perish at death, which is the separation of the spirit and cessation of its attending to the body.

Everything yearns for its own perfection. There is no perfection for man save through invigoration with existence in its entirety, from the level of the First Cause (or Cause of all Causes) to the least existent being, and perception of Divine Majesty such as 'no eye has ever seen, no ear ever heard, and no human heart ever imagined'[01]. He will be thoroughly delighted with this if he is one of the Drawn-Near, for they are near to the Lordly Presence, having entirely shed off their nature. In that they find pure and complete enjoyment, which is termed 'passionate love'.

As for the Righteous, the Godfearing, they are those who keep to the Path leading to the rank of the Drawn-Near by espousing righteous conduct consisting in acquiring knowledge, doing good works, improving their character, acquiring noble traits and thoroughly forsaking base ones—by transforming avarice (for example) into preserving each breath from being squandered, and resentful envy into competing in good works and devotions[02]. Then their low ranks are transformed into lofty ones, for their attributes will have been transformed and their evil works changed into good ones. Their state is one of yearning, for from one point of view it is arrival, yet from another it is absence. Arrival is witnessing. The Drawn-Near have divested themselves of the robes that are their bodies and risen to the World of Holiness (*'Ālam al-Quds*). Their secrets are pure of all that

---

is to resemble Adam to some degree, which implies the acquisition of a substantial degree of nobility of character, wisdom, and spirituality.

01 A reference to the *Ḥadīth* in which God says, *I have prepared for My virtuous servants that which no eye has ever seen, no ear heard, nor mortal heart imagined. Recite if you wish,* **No soul knows what has been prepared for it of repose for the eyes.** (Qur'ān, 32:17) [Bukhārī, *Ṣaḥīḥ*, 3244]. This *ḥadīth* is generally taken to refer to the delights of the Garden, but here the author makes the usual Sufi transposition and applies it at a higher level, that of the contemplation of the Divine Names and Attributes. One can easily see how it applies even more to this higher level.

02 This is the true alchemy: that of transforming the lead of base attributes into the gold of noble ones. Avarice, for instance, is the urge to retain things and not part with them. When transposed to the spiritual level, it becomes a reluctance to part with even one breath without having used it in something spiritually beneficial. Resentful envy, which is anger at someone else's privileges and the wish to see him deprived of them, becomes an urge to surpass him in good works and beneficence.

is not God the Exalted. They perceive that which is indescribable and which the Prophets, may peace be upon them, have perceived before them. They recognize that it is the Supreme Paradise (*Al-Firdaws al-Aʿlā*), for each truth has a reality. Thus it is that they dwell in these Paradises even before dying the common death. **From them they shall never be expelled**[132]. And they are spared the torment of Hell, the reality of which is the love which is the 'origin of every sin'[01] and entirely turning away from God the Exalted—may He be our Refuge.

On the other hand, the experience of torment comes, but only after death has lifted the veils, to those who are heedless and have turned away from God. Then they will told, **Taste the touch of Saqar!**[02] For before that, their feelings had been dulled by the death of their hearts. **Woe to the disbelievers from a severe torment, those who prefer the life of this world to the Hereafter and bar from God's Way, desiring to make it crooked!**[133] Disbelief is to turn away from the Hereafter by concentrating entirely on this world in a manner that corrupts temperaments, preventing them from accepting the truth, for **upon their hearts are covers, so they cannot understand it, and in their ears is wax**[134]. They are veiled and are **dead, not alive, yet they sense it not**[135]. Furthermore, their temperaments become deviant, so that they desire that which is undesirable to the healthy, who are those who love God and follow His Messenger, and it is they who shall be successful **by God's favor and blessing**[136]. **For had it not been for His favor and mercy, not one of you would have been purified; but God purifies whom He will**[137].

O God, pour upon us Your favor and mercy, and grant that we be accepted by You through You, in goodness, faith, constant increase in degree, and satisfaction, **Amid Gardens and a river, in a Sitting-Place of Sincerity, near a Sovereign All-Powerful**[138]. And may God's blessings and peace be upon our Master Muḥammad, the unlettered Prophet, and upon his Family and Companions.

Written on the last day of Jumād al-Awwal of the year 1124 AH[03] by one in need of God's favor and mercy, Aḥmad ibn Zayn al-Ḥabashī, may God grant him to taste what He has granted His saints, and may He take over

01 *The origin of every sin is love of this world. Ḥadīth* in Bayhaqī, *Shuʿab al-īmān* (10501, 10458).

02 Saqar is one of the names of Hell. See Qur'ān, 54:48.

03 *Jumād* being a variant form of *Jumādā*. The date is equivalent to 5th July 1712 CE.

his affairs as He has done theirs. It was written in two sessions, with (. . .)[01]. The impulse arose from a certain book from which [spiritual] assistance was received, supervening upon preparation by the *baraka* of our Shaykh and leader, ʿAbd Allāh ibn ʿAlawī al-Ḥaddād. I believe the title of the book was *Jalā' al-khāṭir*[02].

---

01 A word is missing here.

02 What Ḥabīb Aḥmad ibn Zayn is saying in these lines is that the ground of his soul was prepared by his master, Imām al-Ḥaddād, who taught and trained him, then infused him with spiritual lights, so that when he read *Jalā' al-khāṭir*, a book by Shaykh ʿAbd al-Qādir al-Jīlānī, it provoked in his soul an influx of inspiration, which found him well prepared to receive it and capable of translating it into words and sentences. The result was the present treatise. There are two English translations of *Jalā'* (or *Jilā'*) *al-khāṭir* (or *al-khawāṭir*): *The Removal of Cares* (Jalā' al-Khawāṭir)*: a collection of forty-five discourses*, tr. Muhtar Holland (Fort Lauderdale, FL, 1997); and *Jila' al-Khatir* (Purification of the Mind), ed. M. al-Casnazani al-Husseini, tr. S. al-Dargazelli and L. Fatoohi (Delhi, 1998, etc.; rev. and improved ed., Birmingham, 2008.).

Glossary of Terms

Abdāl. See: *Badal*.

Adhkār. See: *Dhikr*.

Ahl al-Bayt: 'People of the House'. The members of the Prophet Muḥammad's ﷺ immediate family; thereafter, his direct descendants. See also Sayyid, *Sharīf*.

Anṣār. See: Helper.

Aqṭāb. See: *Quṭb*.

'Ārif (pl. *'Ārifūn*), *'Ārif bi-Llāh* ('Gnostic', 'Knower through God'): A person to whom God has granted *Ma'rifa*, which is direct rather than inferential knowledge.(q.v.).

Awliyā'. See: *Walī*.

Awrād. See: *Wird*.

Awtād. See: *Witd*.

Badal (Substitute): One of the *Abdāl*, *Awliyā'* of high rank. Whenever one departs from this life, their place is taken by another. They are sometimes said to number forty.

Bid'a (innovation): The introduction into Islamic belief or practice of something that is new and harmful and is not sanctioned by orthodox doctrine or the Sacred Law.

Book (Arabic: *kitāb*, pl. *kutub*): A Scripture revealed to mankind by God through one of His Messengers (q.v.).

Companion (Arabic: *ṣaḥābī* or *ṣāḥib*, pl. *ṣaḥāba* or *aṣḥāb*): A Muslim man or woman who was privileged to see the Prophet ﷺ in person during his lifetime.

Day (Arabic: *yawm*): A day on Earth is a twenty-four hour cycle of light and darkness caused by the rotation of the earth. It may be a cycle in the subtle dimension, such as the thousand-year-long day it takes the angels to come down from the Divine Presence and return; or a stage unrelated to planetary time as we know it, like the six Days in which God created the universe before the beginning of planetary time. It may also be a period of time the duration of which only God knows, such the Day of Resurrection and Judgement (*yawm al-qiyāma*, *yawm al-dīn*), the length of which, according to some sources, is fifty thousand years according to our reckoning.

Dhikr (pl. *Adhkār*): Invocation, remembrance; the practice of repeating one or more Divine Names, Qur'ānic phrases or verses, or other formulae that are invested by God with *baraka* (q.v.) and are tried and tested means of protection and benefit for the heart.

Emigrant (Arabic: *muhājir*, pl. *muhājirūn*): The title given to those Companions who migrated to Madīna from Makka (or elsewhere), leaving all their immovable property assets behind, to join the Prophet ﷺ and strengthen the nascent Muslim community there.

Emigration (Arabic: *hijra*): The act of migrating to Madīna (see Emigrant). The date of the Prophet's ﷺ migration marks the beginning of the Muslim *Hijrī* era. In this book, dates are given according to the calendar, with the Common Era (CE) equivalent added after a / sign.

Family (Arabic: *āl, bayt*): In the first place, this term denotes literally the members of the Household of the Prophet ﷺ and all his descendants. In the parlance of the Sufis and other lovers of the Prophet ﷺ, his Family extends to all those who sincerely revere him and his wives (the Mothers of the Believers) and his descendants, and strive to follow his example.

Faqīh (pl.: *fuqahā'*): An expert in the Islamic science of *fiqh* (q.v.).

Fatwa (Arabic: *fatwā*, pl. *fatāwā*): A ruling or judgement on a question of Islamic Sacred Law (*Sharī'a*).

Fiqh: Islamic jurisprudence; the science of deriving and interpreting the principles of Sacred Law (*Sharī'a*).

Follower (Arabic: *tābi'*, *tābi'ī*, pl. *tābi'ūn*): A member of the generation of Muslims who inherited through personal contact much of the guidance and blessing of their immediate predecessors, the Companions (q.v.)

Hadith (Arabic: *Ḥadīth*, pl. *Aḥādīth*): A report of something that the Prophet ﷺ said and/or did or assented to; or of something that he tacitly approved by not changing or criticizing it.

Ḥaqīqa (pl. *Ḥaqā'iq*): Invisible truth or reality. It may refer to realities in the spiritual world, to the realities of the Divine Names and Attributes, or to the ultimate reality which is the Divine Essence. Things that at the level of *Ḥaqīqa* are true and just may at times appear paradoxical or even contradictory from the discriminatory perspective of *Sharī'a*.

Helper (Arabic pl.: *anṣār*): The title given to those Companions (q.v.) who were residents of Madīna and made great sacrifices to help the Emigrants establish themselves in their city.

Hypocrite (Arabic: *munāfiq*, pl. *munāfiqūn*): In its specialized meaning this term denotes certain individuals, mainly in the time of the Prophet ﷺ, who professed to be Muslims but who secretly disbelieved and were even prepared to betray him and the Muslims.

Judgment (Arabic: *ḥukm*, pl. *aḥkām*): A ruling of the *Sharī'a* (q.v.) and/or a decision made by a qualified *faqīh* (q.v.) on a point of sacred Law.

Karāma (pl. *Karāmāt*): A supernatural power or action conferred upon a *Walī* by God.

Kashf (unveiling): The direct revelation of things of the Unseen, or of facts not knowable by normal means of cognition or communication.

Kifāya (sufficiency): A collective religious obligation that falls on the entire Muslim community of a given region, all the adult members of which are deemed sinful unless and until it is fulfilled by a sufficient number of individuals, according to the nature of the need to be met.

Madad: Spiritual sustenance, support, or benefit.

Maʿrifa: This word, often translated as 'gnosis', has no satisfactory equivalent in English. It signifies God-given direct knowledge of the Unseen, and particularly of God Most High Himself. *Maʿrifa* is direct awareness in the sense that it comes to the heart unmediated by the processes of the rational mind.

Messenger (Arabic: *Rasūl*, pl. *Rusul*): A human being sent by God with a new Revelation or Scripture (see 'Book'); an Envoy or Emissary to mankind. These terms are more in keeping with the true rank of the *Rusul* than 'Messenger'; but the latter has become familiar in English through long-term and extensive usage. (*Rusul* is also used in some Qur'ānic verses to mean 'angels', the latter word being derived from the Greek *angelos*, 'messenger'.)

Mufti (Arabic: *muftī*): A person whose high level of expertise in *fiqh* (q.v.) makes them qualified to issue fatwas (q.v.).

Nabī. See: Prophet.

Order (Arabic: *ṭarīqa*, pl. *ṭuruq*): A Sufi brotherhood based on adherence to the teachings and Baraka of a particular line of spiritual masters. The word 'Order' in this sense was originally used for Christian monastic brotherhoods.

Path (Arabic: *ṭarīq*, pl. *ṭuruq*): A term for the spiritual journey progressing from distance to closeness to God and knowledge of Him through worship, fear and love of Him.

Prophet (Arabic: *nabī*, pl. *anbiyā'*): A human being sent by God as an Envoy or Emissary: a teacher of the true religion and an exemplar of what a human should be. See also 'Prophethood'.

Prophethood (Arabic: *nubuwwa*): The rank and function of a Prophet (q.v.). Not to be confused with prophecy in the sense of foretelling of a Prophet (q.v.).

Quṭb (*pl. Aqṭāb*): The 'Pole', meaning the *Walī* who is the spiritual Axis of the world. It is widely believed that there is only one *Quṭb* alive in the world at any given time, and that his identity may be unknown to all but a few of mankind.

Sayyid (Arabic: *Sayyid*, pl. *Sāda*, *Sādāt*): Master. A descendant of the Prophet Muḥammad ﷺ; amongst Arabs, the title *Sayyid* is more commonly applied to descendants of Imam Ḥusayn.

Sayyidī: 'my master'. A respectful term of address used amongst Sufis and other pious Muslims.

Sharīʿa: The Islamic Sacred Law, based upon the dictates of the Qur'ān, the Prophetic Sunna, and the judgements of the earliest Imams of the religion as elaborated by trained experts who have mastered the necessary Islamic sciences.

Sharīf (pl. *Shurafā'*), fem.: *Sharīfa*, (pl. *Sharīfāt*): Nobleman/woman. A descendant of the Prophet Muḥammad ﷺ; amongst Arabs, the title *Sharīf* is more commonly applied to descendants of Imam Ḥasan.

Sheikh (Arabic: *Shaykh*, pl. *Mashā'ikh*, *Shuyūkh*): A fully qualified instructor in any of the Islamic sciences; here most often used of the spiritual director of a Sufi Ṭarīqa (q.v.).

Sunna: The lived example—in actions and words—of the Last Prophet ﷺ as preserved and transmitted in Hadiths (q.v.).

Taqwā: Often translated as 'piety' or 'Godfearingness', this word has no satisfactory equivalent in English. To have *taqwā* means to act with awareness that God is aware of one's every action and word. The Prophet ﷺ explained the concept by an image: if you are surrounded by thornbushes, you hold your clothes away from them to avoid tearing them.

Ṭarīqa: This term has three meanings: firstly the Path to the good pleasure and knowledge of God through refining one's soul and the application of a particular methodology; secondly, that methodology itself; thirdly, a named group, or Order (q.v.) of Sufis that follows a particular sheikh (q.v.) with a spiritual genealogy descended ultimately from the Blessed Prophet. The *Ṭarīqa* is sometimes defined as the bridge between the *Sharī'a* and the *Ḥaqīqa* (qq.v.).

Tasbīḥ: Glorification of God Most High, especially in the form of saying *Subḥān Allāh* (Transcendently Perfect is God). According to the Qur'ān, birds and other living creatures each have their own form of *tasbīḥ* which their Creator inspires in them.

Tradition: A saying that imparts wisdom and/or information. In the literature of Islam, 'Tradition' is often, though not always, used as an equivalent to 'Hadith' (q.v.).

Walī (pl. *Awliyā'*); also *Walī Allāh* (pl. *Awliyā' Allāh*): Often translated as 'saint', and sometimes as 'Friend of God', this term (literally meaning 'helper', 'patron', or 'friend') has no satisfactory equivalent in English. A *walī* is a man (and a *waliyya* a woman) whom God has chosen to gain a spiritual rank of special closeness to Him. There are certain *awliyā'* of high rank who have divinely appointed functions in this world. This is a matter of knowledge of the Unseen; and in some cases a person's *wilāya* (q.v.) may be completely concealed from most or even from all of mankind.

Wilāya: The office and function of *walī* (q.v.).

Watad (pl. *Awtād*): 'Peg': One of the *Awtād*, *Awliyā'* of high rank, who help keep the world on an even keel, and of whom there are few in the world at any given time.

Wārid: An influx of divine grace, light, and/or knowledge in response to the devotions (including *Awrād*) of the spiritual seeker.

Wird (pl. *Awrād*): A form of worship that is to be repeated regularly, e.g. once or twice daily or nightly, or after every obligatory prayer. The term is most commonly applied to a form of *dhikr* which the worshipper undertakes to perform as directed by his teacher or master.

Endnotes

1. Abū Dāwūd, *Sunan*, 4607; Tirmidhī, *Sunan*, 2676.
2. Qur'ān, 42:52, 53.
3. Qur'ān, 6:153.
4. Qur'ān, 41:42.
5. Qur'ān, 3:163.
6. Qur'ān, 4:69,70.7
7. Qur'ān, 2:255.8
8. Tirmidhī, *Sunan*, 3148; Ibn Ḥibbān, *Ṣaḥīḥ*, 6242.
9. Qur'ān, 29:69.
10. Qur'ān, 42:13.
11. Qur'ān, 2:285.
12. Qur'ān, 3:81.
13. Qur'ān, 4:163.
14. Qur'ān, 61:153.
15. Qur'ān, 13:11.
16. Qur'ān, 3:31.
17. Qur'ān, 7:156,157.
18. Abū Dāwūd, *Sunan*, 4607; Tirmidhī, *Sunan*, 2676.
19. Qur'ān, 6:153.
20. Qur'ān, 54:7.
21. Qur'ān, 24:54.
22. Qur'ān, 43:13.
23. Qur'ān, 55:26.
24. Qur'ān, 2:105.
25. Qur'an, 10:62, 63.
26. Qur'ān, 46:19.
27. Qur'ān, 46:19 and 58:11.
28. Qur'ān, 83:14, 15.
29. Qur'ān, 59:19.
30. Qur'ān, 5:13.
31. Qur'ān, 4:155.
32. Qur'ān, 31:33.
33. Qur'ān, 3:185.
34. Qur'ān, 39:9.
35. Qur'ān, 32:18.
36. Qur'ān, 45:21.
37. Qur'ān, 6:122.
38. Qur'ān, 7:43.
39. Qur'ān, 49:17.
40. Qur'ān, 49:7,8.
41. Qur'ān, 51:55.
42. Qur'ān, 87:10.
43. Qur'ān, 8:2.
44. Qur'ān, 9:124.
45. Qur'ān, 39:23.
46. Qur'ān, 37:61.
47. *Ḥadīth* [Tirmidhī, *Sunan*, 2681].
48. *Ḥadīth* [Bukhārī, *Ṣaḥīḥ*, 71]
49. *Ḥadīth* [Bukhārī, *Ṣaḥīḥ*, 3382]
50. Qur'ān, 29:69.
51. Qur'ān, 18:28.
52. *Ḥadīth Qudsī* [Bukhārī, *Ṣaḥīḥ*, 6502].
53. Qur'ān, 65:2,3.

54. Qur'ān, 2:282.
55. Qur'ān, 8:29.
56. Qur'ān, 44:31.
57. Qur'ān, 16:8.
58. Qur'ān, 21:23.
59. Qur'ān, 6:149.
60. Qur'ān, 16:60.
61. Qur'ān, 12:76.
62. Qur'ān, 8:17.
63. Qur'ān, 57:3.
64. Qur'ān, 2:210.
65. Qur'ān, 3:19.
66. Qur'ān, 3:85.
67. Qur'ān, 12:108.
68. Bukhārī, *Ṣaḥīḥ*, 2697; Muslim, *Ṣaḥīḥ*, 1718.
69. Ahmad, *Musnad*, 17144; Abū Dāwūd, *Sunan*, 4607.
70. Nasā'ī, *Sunan*, 1578; Ibn Khuzayma, *Ṣaḥīḥ*, 1785.
71. Qur'ān, 4:59.
72. Qur'ān, 17:9.
73. Qur'ān, 20:123.
74. Qur'ān, 2:120.
75. Qur'ān, 7:3.
76. Qur'ān, 16:44.
77. Qur'ān, 53:3–4.
78. Qur'ān, 59:7.
79. Bazzār, *Musnad*, 8993; Dāraquṭnī, *Sunan*, 4606; al-Ḥākim, *Mustadrak*, 319; Bayhaqī, *al-Sunan al-kubrā*, 20337.
80. This is not found in Ḥadīth books but in Ibn ʿAṭiyya, Tafsīr, 1:36; Ibn Ḥayyān, *Tafsīr al-Baḥr al-muḥīṭ*, 1:24.
81. Muslim, *Ṣaḥīḥ*, 867; Ibn Ḥibbān, *Ṣaḥīḥ*, 10.
82. Bukhārī, *Ṣaḥīḥ*, 6101.
83. Tirmidhī, *Sunan*, 2664; Ahmad, *Musnad*, 17174.
84. Qur'ān, 41:42.
85. Qur'ān, 16:89.
86. Qur'ān, 12:111.
87. Qur'ān, 6:38.
88. Qur'ān, 8:29.
89. Qur'ān, 65:3.
90. Qur'ān, 39:22.
91. Qur'ān, 6:122.
92. Bukhārī, *Ṣaḥīḥ*, 52; Muslim, *Ṣaḥīḥ*, 1599.
93. Qur'ān, 24:35.
94. Qur'ān, 24:40.
95. Qur'ān, 58:11.
96. Qur'ān, 47:16.
97. Qur'ān, 16:78.
98. Qur'ān, 35:2.
99. Qur'ān, 42:11.
100. Qur'ān, 6:38.
101. Qur'ān, 12:111.
102. Qur'ān, 6:59.
103. Qur'ān, 4:113.
104. Qur'ān, 2:1–2.
105. Qur'ān, 53:3–4.
106. Qur'ān, 50:37.
107. Qur'ān, 65:12.
108. Qur'ān, 9:118.
109. Qur'ān, 16:28.
110. Qur'ān, 39:18.
111. Qur'ān, 18:82.
112. Qur'ān, 91:7–8.
113. Qur'ān, 41:30.
114. Qur'ān, 10:64.
115. Qur'ān, 8:12.
116. Bukhārī, *Ṣaḥīḥ*, 3469; Muslim, *Ṣaḥīḥ*, 2398.
117. Qur'ān, 22:34.
118. Qur'ān, 65:12. He created so that you, the cause for it, might know His power.

119. Qur'ān, 45:13. He sustains so that you may enjoy what He has subjected to you.
120. Qur'ān, 16:53.
121. Qur'ān, 96:19.
122. Qur'ān, 71:14.
123. Qur'ān, 23:12–13–14.
124. Qur'ān, 95:5.
125. Qur'ān, 16:78.
126. Qur'ān, 20:126.
127. Qur'ān, 20:115.
128. Qur'ān, 67:22.
129. Qur'ān, 20:125.
130. Qur'ān, 95:4.
131. Qur'ān, 20:126.
132. Qur'ān, 15:48.
133. Qur'ān, 14:2–3.
134. Qur'ān, 6:25.
135. Qur'ān, 16:21.
136. Qur'ān, 49:8.
137. Qur'ān, 24:21.
138. Qur'ān, 54:54–55.